Series 79
Exam Secrets
Study Guide

DEAR FUTURE EXAM SUCCESS STORY

First of all, **THANK YOU** for purchasing Mometrix study materials!

Second, congratulations! You are one of the few determined test-takers who are committed to doing whatever it takes to excel on your exam. **You have come to the right place.** We developed these study materials with one goal in mind: to deliver you the information you need in a format that's concise and easy to use.

In addition to optimizing your guide for the content of the test, we've outlined our recommended steps for breaking down the preparation process into small, attainable goals so you can make sure you stay on track.

We've also analyzed the entire test-taking process, identifying the most common pitfalls and showing how you can overcome them and be ready for any curveball the test throws you.

Standardized testing is one of the biggest obstacles on your road to success, which only increases the importance of doing well in the high-pressure, high-stakes environment of test day. Your results on this test could have a significant impact on your future, and this guide provides the information and practical advice to help you achieve your full potential on test day.

Your success is our success

We would love to hear from you! If you would like to share the story of your exam success or if you have any questions or comments in regard to our products, please contact us at **800-673-8175** or **support@mometrix.com**.

Thanks again for your business and we wish you continued success!

Sincerely,
The Mometrix Test Preparation Team

> **Need more help? Check out our flashcards at:**
> **http://MometrixFlashcards.com/Series79**

TABLE OF CONTENTS

Introduction

Thank you for purchasing this resource! You have made the choice to prepare yourself for a test that could have a huge impact on your future, and this guide is designed to help you be fully ready for test day. Obviously, it's important to have a solid understanding of the test material, but you also need to be prepared for the unique environment and stressors of the test, so that you can perform to the best of your abilities.

For this purpose, the first section that appears in this guide is the **Secret Keys**. We've devoted countless hours to meticulously researching what works and what doesn't, and we've boiled down our findings to the five most impactful steps you can take to improve your performance on the test. We start at the beginning with study planning and move through the preparation process, all the way to the testing strategies that will help you get the most out of what you know when you're finally sitting in front of the test.

We recommend that you start preparing for your test as far in advance as possible. However, if you've bought this guide as a last-minute study resource and only have a few days before your test, we recommend that you skip over the first two Secret Keys since they address a long-term study plan.

If you struggle with **test anxiety**, we strongly encourage you to check out our recommendations for how you can overcome it. Test anxiety is a formidable foe, but it can be beaten, and we want to make sure you have the tools you need to defeat it.

Secret Key #1 – Plan Big, Study Small

There's a lot riding on your performance. If you want to ace this test, you're going to need to keep your skills sharp and the material fresh in your mind. You need a plan that lets you review everything you need to know while still fitting in your schedule. We'll break this strategy down into three categories.

Information Organization

Start with the information you already have: the official test outline. From this, you can make a complete list of all the concepts you need to cover before the test. Organize these concepts into groups that can be studied together, and create a list of any related vocabulary you need to learn so you can brush up on any difficult terms. You'll want to keep this vocabulary list handy once you actually start studying since you may need to add to it along the way.

Time Management

Once you have your set of study concepts, decide how to spread them out over the time you have left before the test. Break your study plan into small, clear goals so you have a manageable task for each day and know exactly what you're doing. Then just focus on one small step at a time. When you manage your time this way, you don't need to spend hours at a time studying. Studying a small block of content for a short period each day helps you retain information better and avoid stressing over how much you have left to do. You can relax knowing that you have a plan to cover everything in time. In order for this strategy to be effective though, you have to start studying early and stick to your schedule. Avoid the exhaustion and futility that comes from last-minute cramming!

Study Environment

The environment you study in has a big impact on your learning. Studying in a coffee shop, while probably more enjoyable, is not likely to be as fruitful as studying in a quiet room. It's important to keep distractions to a minimum. You're only planning to study for a short block of time, so make the most of it. Don't pause to check your phone or get up to find a snack. It's also important to **avoid multitasking**. Research has consistently shown that multitasking will make your studying dramatically less effective. Your study area should also be comfortable and well-lit so you don't have the distraction of straining your eyes or sitting on an uncomfortable chair.

 The time of day you study is also important. You want to be rested and alert. Don't wait until just before bedtime. Study when you'll be most likely to comprehend and remember. Even better, if you know what time of day your test will be, set that time aside for study. That way your brain will be used to working on that subject at that specific time and you'll have a better chance of recalling information.

Finally, it can be helpful to team up with others who are studying for the same test. Your actual studying should be done in as isolated an environment as possible, but the work of organizing the information and setting up the study plan can be divided up. In between study sessions, you can discuss with your teammates the concepts that you're all studying and quiz each other on the details. Just be sure that your teammates are as serious about the test as you are. If you find that your study time is being replaced with social time, you might need to find a new team.

Secret Key #2 – Make Your Studying Count

You're devoting a lot of time and effort to preparing for this test, so you want to be absolutely certain it will pay off. This means doing more than just reading the content and hoping you can remember it on test day. It's important to make every minute of study count. There are two main areas you can focus on to make your studying count.

Retention

It doesn't matter how much time you study if you can't remember the material. You need to make sure you are retaining the concepts. To check your retention of the information you're learning, try recalling it at later times with minimal prompting. Try carrying around flashcards and glance at one or two from time to time or ask a friend who's also studying for the test to quiz you.

To enhance your retention, look for ways to put the information into practice so that you can apply it rather than simply recalling it. If you're using the information in practical ways, it will be much easier to remember. Similarly, it helps to solidify a concept in your mind if you're not only reading it to yourself but also explaining it to someone else. Ask a friend to let you teach them about a concept you're a little shaky on (or speak aloud to an imaginary audience if necessary). As you try to summarize, define, give examples, and answer your friend's questions, you'll understand the concepts better and they will stay with you longer. Finally, step back for a big picture view and ask yourself how each piece of information fits with the whole subject. When you link the different concepts together and see them working together as a whole, it's easier to remember the individual components.

Finally, practice showing your work on any multi-step problems, even if you're just studying. Writing out each step you take to solve a problem will help solidify the process in your mind, and you'll be more likely to remember it during the test.

Modality

Modality simply refers to the means or method by which you study. Choosing a study modality that fits your own individual learning style is crucial. No two people learn best in exactly the same way, so it's important to know your strengths and use them to your advantage.

For example, if you learn best by visualization, focus on visualizing a concept in your mind and draw an image or a diagram. Try color-coding your notes, illustrating them, or creating symbols that will trigger your mind to recall a learned concept. If you learn best by hearing or discussing information, find a study partner who learns the same way or read aloud to yourself. Think about how to put the information in your own words. Imagine that you are giving a lecture on the topic and record yourself so you can listen to it later.

For any learning style, flashcards can be helpful. Organize the information so you can take advantage of spare moments to review. Underline key words or phrases. Use different colors for different categories. Mnemonic devices (such as creating a short list in which every item starts with the same letter) can also help with retention. Find what works best for you and use it to store the information in your mind most effectively and easily.

Secret Key #3 – Practice the Right Way

Your success on test day depends not only on how many hours you put into preparing, but also on whether you prepared the right way. It's good to check along the way to see if your studying is paying off. One of the most effective ways to do this is by taking practice tests to evaluate your progress. Practice tests are useful because they show exactly where you need to improve. Every time you take a practice test, pay special attention to these three groups of questions:

- The questions you got wrong
- The questions you had to guess on, even if you guessed right
- The questions you found difficult or slow to work through

This will show you exactly what your weak areas are, and where you need to devote more study time. Ask yourself why each of these questions gave you trouble. Was it because you didn't understand the material? Was it because you didn't remember the vocabulary? Do you need more repetitions on this type of question to build speed and confidence? Dig into those questions and figure out how you can strengthen your weak areas as you go back to review the material.

 Additionally, many practice tests have a section explaining the answer choices. It can be tempting to read the explanation and think that you now have a good understanding of the concept. However, an explanation likely only covers part of the question's broader context. Even if the explanation makes perfect sense, **go back and investigate** every concept related to the question until you're positive you have a thorough understanding.

As you go along, keep in mind that the practice test is just that: practice. Memorizing these questions and answers will not be very helpful on the actual test because it is unlikely to have any of the same exact questions. If you only know the right answers to the sample questions, you won't be prepared for the real thing. **Study the concepts** until you understand them fully, and then you'll be able to answer any question that shows up on the test.

It's important to wait on the practice tests until you're ready. If you take a test on your first day of study, you may be overwhelmed by the amount of material covered and how much you need to learn. Work up to it gradually.

On test day, you'll need to be prepared for answering questions, managing your time, and using the test-taking strategies you've learned. It's a lot to balance, like a mental marathon that will have a big impact on your future. Like training for a marathon, you'll need to start slowly and work your way up. When test day arrives, you'll be ready.

Start with the strategies you've read in the first two Secret Keys—plan your course and study in the way that works best for you. If you have time, consider using multiple study resources to get different approaches to the same concepts. It can be helpful to see difficult concepts from more than one angle. Then find a good source for practice tests. Many times, the test website will suggest potential study resources or provide sample tests.

Practice Test Strategy

If you're able to find at least three practice tests, we recommend this strategy:

UNTIMED AND OPEN-BOOK PRACTICE

Take the first test with no time constraints and with your notes and study guide handy. Take your time and focus on applying the strategies you've learned.

TIMED AND OPEN-BOOK PRACTICE

Take the second practice test open-book as well, but set a timer and practice pacing yourself to finish in time.

TIMED AND CLOSED-BOOK PRACTICE

Take any other practice tests as if it were test day. Set a timer and put away your study materials. Sit at a table or desk in a quiet room, imagine yourself at the testing center, and answer questions as quickly and accurately as possible.

Keep repeating timed and closed-book tests on a regular basis until you run out of practice tests or it's time for the actual test. Your mind will be ready for the schedule and stress of test day, and you'll be able to focus on recalling the material you've learned.

Secret Key #4 – Pace Yourself

Once you're fully prepared for the material on the test, your biggest challenge on test day will be managing your time. Just knowing that the clock is ticking can make you panic even if you have plenty of time left. Work on pacing yourself so you can build confidence against the time constraints of the exam. Pacing is a difficult skill to master, especially in a high-pressure environment, so **practice is vital**.

Set time expectations for your pace based on how much time is available. For example, if a section has 60 questions and the time limit is 30 minutes, you know you have to average 30 seconds or less per question in order to answer them all. Although 30 seconds is the hard limit, set 25 seconds per question as your goal, so you reserve extra time to spend on harder questions. When you budget extra time for the harder questions, you no longer have any reason to stress when those questions take longer to answer.

Don't let this time expectation distract you from working through the test at a calm, steady pace, but keep it in mind so you don't spend too much time on any one question. Recognize that taking extra time on one question you don't understand may keep you from answering two that you do understand later in the test. If your time limit for a question is up and you're still not sure of the answer, mark it and move on, and come back to it later if the time and the test format allow. If the testing format doesn't allow you to return to earlier questions, just make an educated guess; then put it out of your mind and move on.

On the easier questions, be careful not to rush. It may seem wise to hurry through them so you have more time for the challenging ones, but it's not worth missing one if you know the concept and just didn't take the time to read the question fully. Work efficiently but make sure you understand the question and have looked at all of the answer choices, since more than one may seem right at first.

Even if you're paying attention to the time, you may find yourself a little behind at some point. You should speed up to get back on track, but do so wisely. Don't panic; just take a few seconds less on each question until you're caught up. Don't guess without thinking, but do look through the answer choices and eliminate any you know are wrong. If you can get down to two choices, it is often worthwhile to guess from those. Once you've chosen an answer, move on and don't dwell on any that you skipped or had to hurry through. If a question was taking too long, chances are it was one of the harder ones, so you weren't as likely to get it right anyway.

On the other hand, if you find yourself getting ahead of schedule, it may be beneficial to slow down a little. The more quickly you work, the more likely you are to make a careless mistake that will affect your score. You've budgeted time for each question, so don't be afraid to spend that time. Practice an efficient but careful pace to get the most out of the time you have.

Secret Key #5 – Have a Plan for Guessing

When you're taking the test, you may find yourself stuck on a question. Some of the answer choices seem better than others, but you don't see the one answer choice that is obviously correct. What do you do?

The scenario described above is very common, yet most test takers have not effectively prepared for it. Developing and practicing a plan for guessing may be one of the single most effective uses of your time as you get ready for the exam.

In developing your plan for guessing, there are three questions to address:

- When should you start the guessing process?
- How should you narrow down the choices?
- Which answer should you choose?

When to Start the Guessing Process

Unless your plan for guessing is to select C every time (which, despite its merits, is not what we recommend), you need to leave yourself enough time to apply your answer elimination strategies. Since you have a limited amount of time for each question, that means that if you're going to give yourself the best shot at guessing correctly, you have to decide quickly whether or not you will guess.

Of course, the best-case scenario is that you don't have to guess at all, so first, see if you can answer the question based on your knowledge of the subject and basic reasoning skills. Focus on the key words in the question and try to jog your memory of related topics. Give yourself a chance to bring the knowledge to mind, but once you realize that you don't have (or you can't access) the knowledge you need to answer the question, it's time to start the guessing process.

It's almost always better to start the guessing process too early than too late. It only takes a few seconds to remember something and answer the question from knowledge. Carefully eliminating wrong answer choices takes longer. Plus, going through the process of eliminating answer choices can actually help jog your memory.

Summary: Start the guessing process as soon as you decide that you can't answer the question based on your knowledge.

How to Narrow Down the Choices

The next chapter in this book (**Test-Taking Strategies**) includes a wide range of strategies for how to approach questions and how to look for answer choices to eliminate. You will definitely want to read those carefully, practice them, and figure out which ones work best for you. Here though, we're going to address a mindset rather than a particular strategy.

Your odds of guessing an answer correctly depend on how many options you are choosing from.

Number of options left	5	4	3	2	1
Odds of guessing correctly	20%	25%	33%	50%	100%

You can see from this chart just how valuable it is to be able to eliminate incorrect answers and make an educated guess, but there are two things that many test takers do that cause them to miss out on the benefits of guessing:

- Accidentally eliminating the correct answer
- Selecting an answer based on an impression

We'll look at the first one here, and the second one in the next section.

To avoid accidentally eliminating the correct answer, we recommend a thought exercise called **the $5 challenge**. In this challenge, you only eliminate an answer choice from contention if you are willing to bet $5 on it being wrong. Why $5? Five dollars is a small but not insignificant amount of money. It's an amount you could afford to lose but wouldn't want to throw away. And while losing

$5 once might not hurt too much, doing it twenty times will set you back $100. In the same way, each small decision you make—eliminating a choice here, guessing on a question there—won't by itself impact your score very much, but when you put them all together, they can make a big difference. By holding each answer choice elimination decision to a higher standard, you can reduce the risk of accidentally eliminating the correct answer.

The $5 challenge can also be applied in a positive sense: If you are willing to bet $5 that an answer choice *is* correct, go ahead and mark it as correct.

Summary: Only eliminate an answer choice if you are willing to bet $5 that it is wrong.

Which Answer to Choose

You're taking the test. You've run into a hard question and decided you'll have to guess. You've eliminated all the answer choices you're willing to bet $5 on. Now you have to pick an answer. Why do we even need to talk about this? Why can't you just pick whichever one you feel like when the time comes?

The answer to these questions is that if you don't come into the test with a plan, you'll rely on your impression to select an answer choice, and if you do that, you risk falling into a trap. The test writers know that everyone who takes their test will be guessing on some of the questions, so they intentionally write wrong answer choices to seem plausible. You still have to pick an answer though, and if the wrong answer choices are designed to look right, how can you ever be sure that you're not falling for their trap? The best solution we've found to this dilemma is to take the decision out of your hands entirely. Here is the process we recommend:

Once you've eliminated any choices that you are confident (willing to bet $5) are wrong, select the first remaining choice as your answer.

Whether you choose to select the first remaining choice, the second, or the last, the important thing is that you use some preselected standard. Using this approach guarantees that you will not be enticed into selecting an answer choice that looks right, because you are not basing your decision on how the answer choices look.

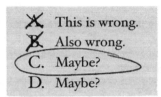

This is not meant to make you question your knowledge. Instead, it is to help you recognize the difference between your knowledge and your impressions. There's a huge difference between thinking an answer is right because of what you know, and thinking an answer is right because it looks or sounds like it should be right.

Summary: To ensure that your selection is appropriately random, make a predetermined selection from among all answer choices you have not eliminated.

Test-Taking Strategies

This section contains a list of test-taking strategies that you may find helpful as you work through the test. By taking what you know and applying logical thought, you can maximize your chances of answering any question correctly!

It is very important to realize that every question is different and every person is different: no single strategy will work on every question, and no single strategy will work for every person. That's why we've included all of them here, so you can try them out and determine which ones work best for different types of questions and which ones work best for you.

Question Strategies

☑ READ CAREFULLY

Read the question and the answer choices carefully. Don't miss the question because you misread the terms. You have plenty of time to read each question thoroughly and make sure you understand what is being asked. Yet a happy medium must be attained, so don't waste too much time. You must read carefully and efficiently.

☑ CONTEXTUAL CLUES

Look for contextual clues. If the question includes a word you are not familiar with, look at the immediate context for some indication of what the word might mean. Contextual clues can often give you all the information you need to decipher the meaning of an unfamiliar word. Even if you can't determine the meaning, you may be able to narrow down the possibilities enough to make a solid guess at the answer to the question.

☑ PREFIXES

If you're having trouble with a word in the question or answer choices, try dissecting it. Take advantage of every clue that the word might include. Prefixes can be a huge help. Usually, they allow you to determine a basic meaning. *Pre-* means before, *post-* means after, *pro-* is positive, *de-* is negative. From prefixes, you can get an idea of the general meaning of the word and try to put it into context.

☑ HEDGE WORDS

Watch out for critical hedge words, such as *likely, may, can, sometimes, often, almost, mostly, usually, generally, rarely,* and *sometimes.* Question writers insert these hedge phrases to cover every possibility. Often an answer choice will be wrong simply because it leaves no room for exception. Be on guard for answer choices that have definitive words such as *exactly* and *always.*

☑ SWITCHBACK WORDS

Stay alert for *switchbacks.* These are the words and phrases frequently used to alert you to shifts in thought. The most common switchback words are *but, although,* and *however.* Others include *nevertheless, on the other hand, even though, while, in spite of, despite,* and *regardless of.* Switchback words are important to catch because they can change the direction of the question or an answer choice.

⊘ FACE VALUE

When in doubt, use common sense. Accept the situation in the problem at face value. Don't read too much into it. These problems will not require you to make wild assumptions. If you have to go beyond creativity and warp time or space in order to have an answer choice fit the question, then you should move on and consider the other answer choices. These are normal problems rooted in reality. The applicable relationship or explanation may not be readily apparent, but it is there for you to figure out. Use your common sense to interpret anything that isn't clear.

Answer Choice Strategies

⊘ ANSWER SELECTION

The most thorough way to pick an answer choice is to identify and eliminate wrong answers until only one is left, then confirm it is the correct answer. Sometimes an answer choice may immediately seem right, but be careful. The test writers will usually put more than one reasonable answer choice on each question, so take a second to read all of them and make sure that the other choices are not equally obvious. As long as you have time left, it is better to read every answer choice than to pick the first one that looks right without checking the others.

⊘ ANSWER CHOICE FAMILIES

An answer choice family consists of two (in rare cases, three) answer choices that are very similar in construction and cannot all be true at the same time. If you see two answer choices that are direct opposites or parallels, one of them is usually the correct answer. For instance, if one answer choice says that quantity x increases and another either says that quantity x decreases (opposite) or says that quantity y increases (parallel), then those answer choices would fall into the same family. An answer choice that doesn't match the construction of the answer choice family is more likely to be incorrect. Most questions will not have answer choice families, but when they do appear, you should be prepared to recognize them.

⊘ ELIMINATE ANSWERS

Eliminate answer choices as soon as you realize they are wrong, but make sure you consider all possibilities. If you are eliminating answer choices and realize that the last one you are left with is also wrong, don't panic. Start over and consider each choice again. There may be something you missed the first time that you will realize on the second pass.

⊘ AVOID FACT TRAPS

Don't be distracted by an answer choice that is factually true but doesn't answer the question. You are looking for the choice that answers the question. Stay focused on what the question is asking for so you don't accidentally pick an answer that is true but incorrect. Always go back to the question and make sure the answer choice you've selected actually answers the question and is not merely a true statement.

⊘ EXTREME STATEMENTS

In general, you should avoid answers that put forth extreme actions as standard practice or proclaim controversial ideas as established fact. An answer choice that states the "process should be used in certain situations, if..." is much more likely to be correct than one that states the "process should be discontinued completely." The first is a calm rational statement and doesn't even make a definitive, uncompromising stance, using a hedge word *if* to provide wiggle room, whereas the second choice is far more extreme.

⊘ BENCHMARK

As you read through the answer choices and you come across one that seems to answer the question well, mentally select that answer choice. This is not your final answer, but it's the one that will help you evaluate the other answer choices. The one that you selected is your benchmark or standard for judging each of the other answer choices. Every other answer choice must be compared to your benchmark. That choice is correct until proven otherwise by another answer choice beating it. If you find a better answer, then that one becomes your new benchmark. Once you've decided that no other choice answers the question as well as your benchmark, you have your final answer.

⊘ PREDICT THE ANSWER

Before you even start looking at the answer choices, it is often best to try to predict the answer. When you come up with the answer on your own, it is easier to avoid distractions and traps because you will know exactly what to look for. The right answer choice is unlikely to be word-for-word what you came up with, but it should be a close match. Even if you are confident that you have the right answer, you should still take the time to read each option before moving on.

General Strategies

⊘ TOUGH QUESTIONS

If you are stumped on a problem or it appears too hard or too difficult, don't waste time. Move on! Remember though, if you can quickly check for obviously incorrect answer choices, your chances of guessing correctly are greatly improved. Before you completely give up, at least try to knock out a couple of possible answers. Eliminate what you can and then guess at the remaining answer choices before moving on.

⊘ CHECK YOUR WORK

Since you will probably not know every term listed and the answer to every question, it is important that you get credit for the ones that you do know. Don't miss any questions through careless mistakes. If at all possible, try to take a second to look back over your answer selection and make sure you've selected the correct answer choice and haven't made a costly careless mistake (such as marking an answer choice that you didn't mean to mark). This quick double check should more than pay for itself in caught mistakes for the time it costs.

⊘ PACE YOURSELF

It's easy to be overwhelmed when you're looking at a page full of questions; your mind is confused and full of random thoughts, and the clock is ticking down faster than you would like. Calm down and maintain the pace that you have set for yourself. Especially as you get down to the last few minutes of the test, don't let the small numbers on the clock make you panic. As long as you are on track by monitoring your pace, you are guaranteed to have time for each question.

⊘ DON'T RUSH

It is very easy to make errors when you are in a hurry. Maintaining a fast pace in answering questions is pointless if it makes you miss questions that you would have gotten right otherwise. Test writers like to include distracting information and wrong answers that seem right. Taking a little extra time to avoid careless mistakes can make all the difference in your test score. Find a pace that allows you to be confident in the answers that you select.

⊘ KEEP MOVING

Panicking will not help you pass the test, so do your best to stay calm and keep moving. Taking deep breaths and going through the answer elimination steps you practiced can help to break through a stress barrier and keep your pace.

Final Notes

The combination of a solid foundation of content knowledge and the confidence that comes from practicing your plan for applying that knowledge is the key to maximizing your performance on test day. As your foundation of content knowledge is built up and strengthened, you'll find that the strategies included in this chapter become more and more effective in helping you quickly sift through the distractions and traps of the test to isolate the correct answer.

Now that you're preparing to move forward into the test content chapters of this book, be sure to keep your goal in mind. As you read, think about how you will be able to apply this information on the test. If you've already seen sample questions for the test and you have an idea of the question format and style, try to come up with questions of your own that you can answer based on what you're reading. This will give you valuable practice applying your knowledge in the same ways you can expect to on test day.

Good luck and good studying!

Copyright © Mometrix Media. You have been licensed one copy of this document for personal use only. Any other reproduction or redistribution is strictly prohibited. All rights reserved.
This content is provided for test preparation purposes only and does not imply an endorsement by Mometrix of any particular political, scientific, or religious point of view.

Collection, Analysis, and Evaluation of Data

PRICE A NEW OFFERING

In order to thoroughly and accurately price a new offering, the data that needs to be considered includes the following:

1. The current direction of the market overall
2. The trends of the underlying sector
3. The financial well-being of the company, both of its own merits as well as in comparison to its competitors
4. Annual and quarterly reports made publicly available by the company
5. Financial statements and proxies required by regulatory organizations

FORM 8-K, FORM 6-K, FORM 10-K, FORM 10-KSB, FORM 10-Q, AND FORM 10-QSB

1. Form 8-K is filed any time a company needs to report changes of material importance to shareholders or the Securities & Exchange Commission (SEC).
2. Form 6-K is specifically used by issuers of foreign securities. This required form is used to report any information that is submitted to the company's local securities regulators in between quarterly or annual financial reports submitted to the SEC.
3. Form 10-K is an annual filing that is required to be submitted within 60 days of the end of a company's fiscal year. This filing is typically very detailed, containing both organizational information (such as current structure) and financial information (outstanding shares, underlying holdings, earnings, etc.)
4. Form 10-10KSB is an annual filing that is required to be submitted within 90 days of the end of a company's fiscal year. This form is similar to a 10-K, but it is used by small businesses (penny stocks for the most part), hence the SB in the title.
5. Form 10-Q is a quarterly filing that is required to be submitted within 40 days of the end of the first three fiscal quarters. This form provides an up-to-date disclosure of the company's performance.
6. Form 10-QSB is a quarterly filing that is required to be submitted within 45 days of the end of the first three fiscal quarters for a small business (penny stocks for the most part), hence the SB in the title.

FILING A PRELIMINARY PROXY STATEMENT

A company is required to provide the Securities & Exchange Commission (SEC) with its proxy statement at least 10 days prior to the date upon which it will be made available to shareholders. However, if the only information contained within the proxy deals with any of the following information, this requirement will be waived:

1. Board of directors elections
2. Approval of a company's accountants
3. Shareholder proposal (e.g., approving a slate of directors)
4. Executive compensation approval

5. Proposal to continue an advisory arrangement that was included in a previous proxy filing (this is for investment or business development companies)
6. Proposal to increase the number of shares to be issued (for open-end investment companies)

BENEFICIAL OWNER

In general, owning greater than 10 percent of the outstanding shares of a company's stock results in being defined as an *insider* and being subject to certain restrictions involving the disposition of the stock. The term *beneficial owner* implies that an individual or organization owns the shares of a company's stock for the benefit of other individuals. When this occurs, even if the aggregate number of shares held by that individual or the organization exceeds 10 percent of the company's outstanding shares, the dispositive restrictions will not be enforced. An example of this concept is when a pension plan holds shares in a pool for the benefit of many employees.

PECUNIARY INTEREST AND INDIRECT PECUNIARY INTEREST

Pecuniary interest indicates that the beneficial owner of a company's shares has the ability to profit from transactions involving that stock. *Indirect pecuniary interest* occurs when the beneficial owner profits from the transactions but not through any direct action. Examples include holding shares of the stock in a trust or owning derivative securities (even if they are not currently exercisable).

PROHIBITED RELATIONSHIP BETWEEN RESEARCH ANALYSTS AND INVESTMENT BANKING PERSONNEL

In order to ensure that the reports created by research analysts are not inappropriately tainted and that the analysts are not encouraged to report a more favorable impression of a company's overall well-being, a member of the investment banking department may not supervise a research analyst. In addition, the compensation or performance evaluations may not be overseen or influenced by an individual working in the investment banking department.

RESEARCH REPORTS

CONFIRMING RESEARCH REPORT INFORMATION

Should a research analyst want to confirm certain information is accurate prior to publishing a research report, specific sections may be sent to the subject company, but the following precautions must be taken:

1. The draft of the report must be submitted to the analyst's legal department prior to sending any sections to the subject company.
2. The sections submitted to the subject company cannot include the overall summary, rating, or price target
3. If the subject company provides countering information to the research analyst that alters the overall summary, rating, or price target, the analyst must submit a written opinion to the legal department justifying the changes.

RESTRICTION INVOLVING PUBLISHING RESEARCH REPORTS

If a company is the sponsor or co-sponsor of an initial public offering, the company may not release any research reports for 40 calendar days following the date of the offering. Additionally, if a company is the sponsor or co-sponsor of a secondary offering, the company may not release any research reports for 10 calendar days following the date of that offering.

TRADING RESTRICTIONS FOR THE RELEASE OF A RESEARCH REPORT

The following trading restrictions must be followed by research analysts when a research report publication is pending:

1. Research analysts may not receive shares before the initial public offering if the issuer's principal business is the same as any subject company followed by the analyst.
2. Research analysts may not trade in any security issued by a subject company that they follow beginning 30 days before the publication of a research report involving that company and ending five days after the publication without specific consent from their legal department.
3. Research analysts may not buy or sell any security issued by a subject company they follow if the transaction would not be in keeping with the rating from their most recently published research report.

DISCLOSING A CONFLICT OF INTEREST

A research analyst must disclose a conflict of interest in the following scenarios:

1. If the analyst or a member of the household has a financial interest in the company (the disclosure must include the nature of the interest)
2. If the analyst owned 1 percent or more of the outstanding shares of the company as of the end of the month prior to the publication of the report (or the end of the second-most recent month if the report will be dated prior to the 10th of the month)
3. Any other conflict of interest known by the research analyst

TYPES OF COMPENSATION DISCLOSED IN RESEARCH REPORTS

Research analysts must disclose the following sources of compensation in their research reports:

1. Any compensation that is based upon the company's investment banking revenue
2. Any compensation from the subject company in the past 12 months
3. Any compensation that the research analyst expects to receive the from the subject company in the next three months

BALANCE SHEET

A balance sheet is considered a snapshot of the company's net worth or financial condition. It is analyzed to determine if the company has a capital surplus or a deficit. The report is broken down into three sections: assets, liabilities, and stockholder's equity.

The assets section contains current assets (cash, accounts receivable, prepaid items, and inventory), depreciable assets (property, buildings, and equipment), and intangible assets (good will and trade names). The liabilities section contains current liabilities (interest due on notes, accounts payable, taxes that are owed in the short term, and unearned revenues), and long-term liabilities (bonds payable and long-term loans). The stockholder's equity section is the sum of common stock and retained earnings less any treasury stock.

INCOME STATEMENT

An income statement is used to indicate how a company performed over a specific accounting time period. The performance is broken down into operating and nonoperating activities. The income statement is also known as a profit and loss statement.

The operating activities section includes only revenues and expenses that are a direct result of normal business operations. The expenses include cost of goods sold, selling, general and administrative expenses, and depreciation (including depletion and amortization). The nonoperating activities section is used to report revenues and expenses related to items that are not tied to the company's normal business operations. For example, if an organization purchased a warehouse to hold its goods and sold off the equipment that was contained in the warehouse at the time of possession, this revenue would be considered nonoperating.

CASH FLOW STATEMENT

A cash flow statement is created by taking specific information from the balance sheet and the income statement to determine how the company is running from an operations perspective, including where money is coming from and how it is being spent. The statement is broken down into three sections: operations, investing, and financing.

The operations section provides details as to how much cash is brought in directly from sales of a company's goods or services. The investing section details changes in cash position as a result of buying or selling equipment or other hard assets. The financing section details changes in debt and dividends.

LIQUIDITY

Liquidity can also be called *marketability*. It is a measure of how quickly an asset can be sold in the market without reducing the price. The liquidity ratios that are used most often include the current ratio, the quick ratio, and the cash ratio.

The current ratio equals: $\dfrac{\text{current assets}}{\text{current liabilities}}$

The result indicates to what degree the company can pay its short-term debts with cash on hand. This ratio is also known as *working capital*.

The quick ratio equals: $\dfrac{\text{cash equivalents}+\text{short}-\text{term investments}+\text{accounts receivable}}{\text{current liabilities}}$

This ratio is more conservative than the current ratio because it does not include assets that are more difficult to turn into cash. The quick ratio is also known as the *acid test ratio*.

The most conservative ratio is the cash ratio, which equals: $\dfrac{\text{cash}+\text{equivalents}+\text{invested funds}}{\text{current liabilities}}$

DEBT-TO-CAPITAL, DEBT-TO-EQUITY AND RECEIVABLES TURNOVER

1. Debt-to-capital measures a company's leverage through debt. Here is the formula:

$$\frac{\text{the company's debt, including both short and long term obligations}}{\text{shareholder equity} + \text{debt}}$$

2. Debt-to-equity measures a company's leverage through equity. Here is the formula:

$$\frac{\text{the company's liabilities}}{\text{shareholders' equity}}$$

3. Receivables turnover measures how quickly and efficiently a company is able to collect outstanding debts, which are in essence interest-free loans. Here is the formula:

$$\frac{\text{net credit sales}}{\text{average accounts receivable}}$$

INVENTORY TURNOVER AND PAYABLES TURNOVER

1. *Inventory turnover* measures how many times an inventory is sold and subsequently replaced over a specific time period. There are two different formulas that can be used.

$$\frac{\text{sales}}{\text{inventory}}$$

and

$$\frac{\text{cost of goods sold}}{\text{average inventory}}$$

2. *Payables turnover* measures the pace at which a company pays its debts to suppliers. Here is the formula:

$$\frac{\text{total supplier purchases}}{\text{average accounts payable}}$$

PROFITABILITY, EBITDA AND EBITDAR

Profitability is the extent to which a company is able to generate earnings over its expenses during the same time period. *EBITDA* is earnings before interest, taxes, depreciation, and amortization. The formula is self-explanatory. It is often used to compare profitability between companies that may choose to finance their organizations through different means or choose a different accounting method. *EBITDAR* is earnings before interest, taxes, depreciation, amortization, and restructuring or rent costs. This method of measuring earnings is often used by organizations that have large rent costs, such as a restaurant, or those that have recently undergone restructuring, which is considered a one-time expense.

EARNINGS PER SHARE (EPS) AND EARNINGS YIELD AND EQUITY TURNOVER

1. *Earnings per share (EPS)* is a measure of how much profit can be allocated to each outstanding share of stock. Here is the formula:

$$\frac{\text{net income} - \text{dividends on preferred stock}}{\text{average outstanding shares}}$$

2. *Earnings yield* is the inverse of the price-earnings (P/E) ratio. It illustrates the percentage of each dollar invested in the stock that was earned by the company. Here is the formula:

$$\frac{\text{earnings per share}}{\text{current market price}}$$

3. *Equity turnover* is a measurement of how well a company is able to create sales given its equity investment (common stock and preferred stock included).

   Here is the formula:

$$\frac{\text{net sales}}{\text{average total equity}}$$

OPERATING MARGIN AND NET MARGIN

1. *Operating margin* is a ratio that is used to determine the appropriateness of a company's pricing strategy and to what degree it is able to pay for variable costs including wages and materials. Here is the formula:

$$\frac{\text{operating income}}{\text{net sales}}$$

2. *Net margin* is a ratio that demonstrates how much of each dollar the company earns is turned into profits. Here is the formula:

$$\frac{\text{net profit (defined as revenue} - \text{cost of goods sold (COGS)} - \text{operating expenses} - \text{interest} - \text{taxes}}{\text{revenue}}$$

RETURN ON ASSETS (ROA), RETURN ON EQUITY (ROE) AND RETURN ON INVESTMENT (ROI)

1. *Return on assets (ROA)* measures how profitable a company is in relation to the company's assets. In other words, it looks at how well the company uses assets to create earnings. Here is the formula:

$$\frac{\text{net income}}{\text{total assets}}$$

2. *Return on equity (ROE)* looks at how well a company profits with the money that has been invested by means of shareholders. Here is the formula:

$$\frac{\text{net income}}{\text{shareholders' equity}}$$

3. *Return on investment (ROI)* is a measurement of what benefit an investor receives given the cost of the underlying investment. Here is the formula:

$$\frac{\text{gain from investment} - \text{cost of investment}}{\text{cost of investment}}$$

RETURN ON INVESTMENT CAPITAL (ROIC) AND TOTAL EXPENSE RATIO (TER)

1. *Return on investment capital (ROIC)* measures how efficiently a company uses the capital at its disposable to create profit. Here is the formula:

$$\frac{\text{net income} - \text{dividends}}{\text{total capital}}$$

2. *Total expense ratio (TER)* is associated with investment funds. It measures total costs (management fees, trading fees, and operational expenses) as a function of the total assets of the fund so that an investor knows what the true return on the investment is. Here is the formula:

$$\frac{\text{total funds costs}}{\text{total fund assets}}$$

LEVERAGE AND RATIOS: INTEREST COVERAGE AND DEBT TO EBITDA

The term *leverage* is the amount of debt used to finance a project or an organization.

1. *Interest coverage* is a ratio that determines the extent to which an organization can pay the interest owed on outstanding debt. Here is the formula:

$$\frac{\text{earnings before interest and taxes}}{\text{interest expense}}$$

2. *Debt to EBITDA* is a ratio that takes into consideration the fact that a company can decrease its debt. This ratio shows how many years it would take to pay back debt if both debt and EBITDA remain the same.

ACCRETION/DILUTION, ENTERPRISE VALUE AND ADJUSTED EV/EBITDA

1. *Accretion/dilution* is used when there is a merger or acquisition on the table. The purpose is to project how the acquisition will affect the earnings per share of the acquirer. The acquirer can then compare the new earnings per share to what it would be if they choose not to act upon the acquisition.
2. *Enterprise value* is a measure of a company's value. It is a quick valuation to determine starting value for a potential takeover bid. The formula is this: market capitalization + debt + minority interest + preferred shares – total cash and cash equivalents.
3. *Adjusted EV/EBITDA* is a valuation tool that can be used to compare companies with different capital structures. Regardless of whether a company used equity or debt to raise capital, EBITDA remains effectively unchanged, making it a fair tool to compare two companies.

PRICE TO BOOK VALUE AND COMPOUND ANNUAL GROWTH RATE (CAGR)

1. *Price to book value* is a ratio that is used to compare the market value of a stock to its book value. It is also known as the *price-equity ratio*.

   Here is the formula:

$$\frac{\text{closing price of the stock}}{\text{latest quarter's book value per share}}$$

2. *Compound annual growth rate (CAGR)* is the growth rate year-over-year for a specific investment. It allows an investor to imagine what an investment would have grown to if it grew at a steady rate over a certain number of years. Here is the formula:

$$\left(\frac{\text{Ending Value}}{\text{Beginning Value}}\right)^{\frac{1}{\text{\# of years}}} - 1$$

COST OF CAPITAL

Cost of capital is the total cost of the all funds used to finance an organization. It takes into consideration both equity and debt financing. Calculating this is a multiple-step process:

Step 1: The formula for the cost of debt financing is this: yield to maturity of debt x (1 – T), where T is the company's marginal tax rate.

Step 2: The formula for the cost of equity financing is found using the capital asset pricing model (CAPM): risk-free rate of return + (the company's beta X risk premium)

Step 3: Determine the ratio of debt to total financing and equity to total financing

Step 4: Multiply each ratio by its respective cost.

DIVIDEND DISCOUNT MODEL AND DIVIDEND PAYOUT RATIO

1. The *dividend discount model* is one that values the price of a particular stock by using the expected future dividends and discounting them back to find the present value. An investor would use the result to determine whether the stock is under or overvalued. Here is the formula:

$$\frac{\text{dividend per share}}{\text{discount rate} - \text{dividend growth rate}}$$

2. The *dividend payout ratio* is a percentage measuring the earnings paid to shareholders in the form of dividends. Here is the formula:

$$\frac{\text{yearly dividend per share}}{\text{earnings per share}}$$

DIVIDEND YIELD AND ENTERPRISE VALUE TO SALES

1. The *dividend yield* is a ratio that is used to determine how much a company pays out in the form of dividends each year in relation to the stock price. Here is the formula:

$$\frac{\text{annual dividends per share}}{\text{price per share}}$$

2. The *enterprise value to sales* measures the value of an organization to the organization's sales. This helps potential buyers of the organization know how much it would cost to buy the sales. Here is the formula:

$$\frac{\text{market cap} + \text{debt} + \text{preferred shares} - \text{cash and cash equivalents}}{\text{annual sales}}$$

FORWARD P/E, INTERNAL RATE OF RETURN (IRR) AND LAST TWELVE MONTHS (LTM) P/E

1. *Forward P/E* looks at the price-to-earnings ratio using a forecasted earnings estimate. Here is the formula:

$$\frac{\text{market price per share}}{\text{expected earnings per share}}$$

2. *Internal rate of return (IRR)* allows an investor to look at projects side by side and determine the growth each is expected to create. It is also known as *net present value calculation*.
3. *Last twelve months (LTM) P/E* is also known as a trailing twelve months P/E. It is the shortest period of time that most investors believe provides enough meaningful data to evaluate a company's results.

MARKET CAPITALIZATION, NORMALIZED OPERATING EARNINGS AND PRICE TO CASH FLOW

1. *Market capitalization* is the total value of all outstanding shares. Here is the formula: total number of outstanding shares x current market price.
2. *Normalized operating earnings* is the earnings for an organization taking into consideration the cyclical ups and downs of the economy and unusual nonrecurring items.
3. *Price to cash flow* is a measure of a stock price to the cash flow on a per-share basis. Here is the formula:

$$\frac{\text{share price}}{\text{cash flow per share}}$$

PRICE TO EARNINGS AND PRICE TO FREE CASH FLOW

1. *Price to earnings* is a measure of a company's current share price, compared to the per-share earnings, to indicate whether investors are expecting high or low future growth. This is also known as a *price multiple* or an *earnings multiple*.

Here is the formula:

$$\frac{\text{market value per share}}{\text{earnings per share}}$$

2. *Price to free cash flow* is a measure of a company's price to its annual free cash flow. Investors use this to determine how expensive a company is considered. Here is the formula:

$$\frac{\text{market capitalization}}{\text{free cash flow}}$$

PRICE TO EARNINGS TO GROWTH (PEG RATIO) AND PRICE TO SALES

1. *Price to earnings to growth (PEG ratio)* is a measure of a stock's value while also considering the company's earnings growth. It allows investors to determine whether a stock is potentially undervalued. Here is the formula:

$$\frac{\text{P/E ratio}}{\text{annual earnings per share (EPS)growth}}$$

2. *Price to sales* is a measure of a stock's price relative to the company's revenues. Here is the formula:

$$\frac{\text{current share price}}{\text{sales per share}}$$

SUM OF THE PARTS ANALYSIS, STOCK VOLATILITY AND BETA

1. *Sum of the parts analysis* is a measure of what a company would be worth if all of its underlying divisions were broken up and spun off into separate companies or acquired by another organization. In many cases, an organization may be worth more this way than sold as one large company.

2. *Stock volatility* is a statistical term and refers to the amount of change in the price of a stock. It is measured in the form of standard deviation and then compared to the returns of its comparable index or competitor.
3. *Beta* is also known as *systematic risk*. It is a comparison of the risk of a security, an industry, or a portfolio against the market as a whole.

TWO MOST COMMON TYPES OF INVENTORY ASSET-MANAGEMENT SYSTEMS

The two most common types of inventory asset-management systems are last in first out (LIFO) and first in, first out (FIFO). *LIFO* presumes that the assets made or purchased last are the first ones sold or used. *FIFO* presumes that the assets made or purchased first are the first ones sold or used. A company chooses which system they want to use at the time of formation.

FINANCIAL MARKET, MONEY MARKET AND DERIVATIVE MARKET

1. A *financial market* is a general term relating to any marketplace where one can buy or sell assets. Financial markets are in almost every nation in the world and drastically vary in size and offerings.
2. A *money market* is a financial instrument that consists of a variety of short-term securities. The maturity varies from a few days to just under one year. Certificates of deposit (CDs), treasury bills, commercial paper, municipal notes, banker's acceptances, and repurchase agreements are all included in money market instruments. While a money market is often considered a cash equivalent, there is a risk of default.
3. A *derivative market* is a marketplace where derivative securities are exchanged. A *derivative* is a security contract where the value is derived from the underlying assets. The most common types of derivatives include options, forwards, and futures.

INTERBANK MARKET, PRIMARY MARKET, SECONDARY MARKET, AND OVER-THE-COUNTER (OTC) MARKET

1. An *interbank market* is a marketplace where financial institutions including banks trade currencies. The largest interbank market is called the *forex market.*
2. A *primary market* is a marketplace for the issuance of new securities. The purchase of these securities comes directly from the issuer rather than from another investor.
3. A secondary market is a marketplace where securities are bought and sold from other investors rather than from the issuer directly.
4. An *over-the-counter (OTC) market* is a marketplace where stocks that are not listed on one of the three main stock exchanges (Nasdaq, New York Stock Exchange [NYSE], or American Stock Exchange [AMEX]) are traded. The majority of the stocks traded OTC are penny stocks.

MACROECONOMICS, MICROECONOMICS AND SCARCITY

1. *Macroeconomics* looks at large-scale factors that affect a country on the whole, such as the gross domestic product, the allocation of natural resources, and prevailing interest rates.
2. *Microeconomics* looks at smaller factors that impact organizations and individuals, such as supply and demand and how changes in prices impact the two.
3. *Scarcity* is the core of all economic decisions. It is the idea that there is a limited amount of resources, including land, labor, and capital, to meet the unlimited desires of people.

BUSINESS CYCLE, RECESSION AND DEPRESSION

1. A *business cycle* comprises the changes or fluctuations that are experienced in an economy over a period of time. The cycle is made of a series of expansions and contractions.
2. A *recession* is an economic downturn that is temporary in nature. A recession is trademarked by a decline in gross domestic product (GDP), industrial production, and retail sales and a rise in unemployment over two successive quarters.
3. A *depression* is an economic downturn over an extended period of time. In general, an economy will be labeled a recession until the point in time where GDP declines by greater than 10 percent.

MICRO-CAP, SMALL CAP, MID CAP, LARGE CAP, AND MARKET INDEX

1. A *micro-cap* stock is a publicly traded company characterized by a market capitalization between $50 million and $300 million.
2. A *small-cap* stock is a publicly traded company characterized by a market capitalization between $300 million and $2 billion.
3. A *mid-cap* stock is a publicly traded company characterized by a market capitalization between $2 billion and $10 billion.
4. A *large-cap* stock is a publicly traded company characterized by a market capitalization more than $10 billion.
5. A *market index* is a benchmark, a comparative tool that allows investors to determine how their securities have performed over a period of time. The benchmark comprises several securities with similar traits and market capitalizations.

LEADING INDICATOR, COINCIDENT INDICATOR AND LAGGING INDICATOR

1. A *leading indicator* is a factor that can be used to predict a change in the economy. An example of a leading indicator is the slope on the bond yield curve. For example, when longer-term duration bonds do not offer much (if any) additional yield over short-term bonds, this can be an indicator of an economic downturn.
2. A *coincident indicator* is a factor that can be used to indicate the current status of the economy within a particular area. These are things that generally move in step with the economy. An example is gross domestic product because it illustrates the value of all goods and services provided during the year.
3. A *lagging indicator* is a factor that only changes after the economy has moved in a particular direction. An example is the unemployment rate because, in general, companies lay off employees after an economic downturn has already begun.

FISCAL POLICY AND MONETARY POLICY

Fiscal policy is the use of revenue collection (i.e., taxes) and government spending in order to impact the overall economy. *Monetary policy* involves controlling the supply of money in order to achieve a target interest rate that is believed will bring about economic stability or growth. Economists and legislators use these two policies to attempt to accomplish certain economic outcomes and influence the direction of the markets.

INFLATION AND DEFLATION

Inflation is a measure of how rapidly the prices of goods and services available in an economy increase over a given period of time. Therefore, an increase in the inflation rate indicates a quicker increase in the price; in general, people have less to spend, and the economy tends to slow. When there is a decrease in the inflation rate, there is still an increase in the price; it is just at a slower pace. *Deflation* is when the price of goods and services falls.

INTEREST RATES AND INFLATION

In general, interest rates and inflation have an inverse relationship, meaning that the central bank raises interest rates in an attempt to decrease inflation and lowers the interest rates to promote economic growth. While higher interest rates imply that investors will get higher rates of return on bank account deposits; it also means that homeowners and organizations make higher mortgage payments on the properties they own.

ROLE OF THE CENTRAL BANKS

The central bank is the regulatory authority for a country's monetary policy. Its main role is to provide stability to the country's currency system by buying and selling government instruments in the market. However, another role of the central bank is to be the lender of last resort. When the economy is said to be normal, banks will lend money to one another at the prevailing federal funds rate. When the banking system is failing and banks will not lend money to one another, they look to the central bank to cover their shortages at the current discount rate.

INTEREST RATES IMPACT THE PRICES OF BONDS

Interest rates and bond prices have an inverse relationship, meaning that, as interest rates rise, bond prices fall and vice versa. To explain this concept, assume that an investor owns a 10-year bond with an interest rate of 5 percent. The face value of the bond is $1,000. The market value (what an investor is willing to pay to buy the bond) of the bond depends entirely on the prevailing interest rate. If the current interest rate is higher than 5 percent (7 percent for example), an investor is going to expect a discount on the price as he or she will not be willing to pay $1,000 for a bond that is paying less than other bonds available in the marketplace. If on the other hand, the current interest rate is lower (e.g., 3 percent), an investor is going to be willing to pay a premium for the bond.

INTEREST RATES IMPACT THE STOCK MARKET

Interest rate and stock prices have an inverse relationship, meaning that, as interest rates rise, stock prices fall and vice versa. To explain this concept, let's assume that the Fed increases the federal funds rate from 5 to 8 percent. This increase will impact individuals, particularly those with credit card debt with variable interest rates and those with adjustable rate mortgages. In essence, overnight these individuals have less money to spend and as a result spend less on goods and services. As a result, the revenue of many businesses declines. In addition, because businesses also have loans, their interest expenses increase. As a result of these two components, their bottom-line profits are less, thereby impacting a number of key ratios that investors look at when determining the appropriate valuation of a company's stock price.

COMMON STOCK AND PREFERRED STOCK

1. *Common stock* is an equity security constituting ownership of the organization. Someone who owns common stock helps determine who is on the board of directors and approves corporate policy, both via elections. In the event of a company filing bankruptcy and its assets being liquidated, common stockholders are compensated for their investment last, only after preferred stockholders and debt holders are paid in full.
2. *Preferred stock* is an equity security constituting ownership of the organization. Preferred stockholders are paid fixed dividends ahead of common stockholders, and in the event of the company filing bankruptcy, preferred stockholders are paid before common stockholders. However, preferred stockholders generally do not have voting rights.

RIGHTS AND WARRANTS

1. *Rights* are securities that entitle stockholders to buy new shares issued by a company at a preset price. The price is usually less than what they would pay in the market, and the number of shares they can purchase is in direct proportion to the number of rights owned. Rights are only available for a brief time period, after which they expire.

2. *Warrants* are derivative securities that entitle a debt holder to buy a specific number of new shares issued by a company at a preset price over a specific (long-term) period of time.

EMPLOYEE STOCK OPTIONS AND STOCK APPRECIATION RIGHTS (SARs)

1. *Employee stock options* are considered a part of an employee's compensation package. In many cases, the use of stock options is reserved for company executives and directors. An employee stock option gives the employee the right to buy a specific number of shares at a specific price (i.e., the strike price) beginning at a specific point in the future, known as the *vesting date*. Sometimes the options vest over a period of years, for example, 25 percent per year beginning one year from the date they were initially granted. The right to exercise the option expires at a specific point in time, usually 10 years after the grant is made (unless the employee terminates his or her employment before such time, in which case the options are generally forfeited barring a clause in the employee's contract. The employee would choose to exercise the option only if the strike price (the amount he or she pays for the shares) is less than what they would pay were they to buy the shares on the open market.

2. *Stock appreciation rights (SARs)* behave essentially the same way as employee stock options. The main difference is that, instead of the employee having to actually pay the strike price, the employee will receive the difference between the current fair market value price at the time of exercise and the strike price in either the form of cash or stock.

AMERICAN DEPOSITARY RECEIPTS (ADRs) AND GLOBAL DEPOSITARY RECEIPTS (GDRs)

1. *American depositary receipts (ADRs)* are financial instruments that are issued by banks and constitute a foreign company's publicly traded securities. In essence, a custodian bank in the foreign country holds the shares of the stock, and a depositary receipt is what is traded on the local exchange. The ADR can be sponsored, meaning that there is a legal relationship between the ADR and the foreign company that covers the cost of issuing the equity and is permitted on any of the major exchanges. Unsponsored ADRs may only be traded on the over-the counter (OTC) market.

2. *Global depositary receipts (GDRs)* behave in the same fashion as ADRs. The main difference is that GDRs are traded in foreign markets such as Singapore and London.

CORPORATE BOND AND MORTGAGE BOND

1. A *corporate bond* is a debt instrument that is issued by a company and sold directly to investors. In exchange for the investment, the company will pay a stated coupon rate (interest payment) at predetermined intervals over the course of the bond, leading up to the repayment of the principal at the end of the term. In the event of dissolution of the company, debt holders are repaid before stockholders.

2. A *mortgage bond* is a bond that is secured by at least one (but usually several) mortgages. Because the mortgage is tied to actual real estate, in the event of a default, the underlying real estate could be sold to cover the debt. Therefore, the main risks involved with this type of investment are interest rate risk (if rates drop, the mortgage may be refinanced, and therefore, the mortgage would be paid back sooner) and the risk that housing prices fall to a point where the sale of the property would not cover the debt in its entirety.

DEBENTURE, CONVERTIBLE BOND AND CALLABLE BOND

1. A *debenture* is a type of debt instrument that is not tied to any specific assets. They are sold based solely on the solid reputation and creditworthiness of the issuer. These can be issued by both corporations and governments.
2. A *convertible bond* is a type of bond that can be converted to a specific preset number of shares of stock at certain points in time at the discretion of the holder of the bond.
3. A *callable bond* is one that gives the issuer of the bond the ability to repurchase the bond over the course of its life, usually after a certain period of time has passed. In general, a company will only elect to call a bond if interest rates have dropped below the stated coupon rate of a previously issued bond.

COLLATERAL TRUST BOND, EQUIPMENT TRUST OBLIGATION, GUARANTEED BOND, AND ASSET-BACKED SECURITY

1. A collateral trust bond is one that is backed by a specific asset, usually stock or other bonds. The assets that secure the bond are held in trust for the benefit of the bondholders.
2. An equipment trust obligation is similar to a collateral trust bond; the main difference is that the collateral backing the bond is specific physical equipment rather than an intangible asset.
3. A guaranteed bond is one that provides the bondholder with a secondary guarantee that the interest and the principal will be paid by a third party if the issuer should ever default on the payments.
4. An asset-backed security is a debt security that is backed by a loan, lease, or receivables of a company. It does not include mortgage or real estate, which fall under other categories.

EUROBOND, VARIABLE RATE BOND AND ZERO COUPON RATE BOND

1. A Eurobond is one that is issued in a different currency than the one used in the country in which the bond was issued.
2. A variable rate bond is one where the underlying interest rate, which determines the amount of the coupon payment, is adjusted at various points in time. The bond can be redeemed upon request of the bondholder.
3. A zero coupon rate bond is one that does not make coupon payments during the life of the bond. Instead, at the time of maturity, the bondholder will receive the principal and all accrued interest in one lump-sum payment.

CONVEXITY, MAKE-WHOLE PROVISION, PAR VALUE, PREMIUM, DISCOUNT, AND CONVERSION RATIO

1. *Convexity* is a measure in the curvature between bond prices and bond yields that helps investors see how duration changes in relation to interest rate changes, so they better understand how much market risk their bond portfolio is subject to.
2. The *make-whole provision* allows the borrower to pay off all remaining debt before the date of maturity. However, the borrower must calculate the net present value of the remaining stream of coupon payments in order to compensate the investor for the payments they would have received had the bond not been called.
3. *Par value* is the face value of the bond; in other words, it is the stated value of the bond.
4. *Premium* is a way to say that the current price of the bond is higher than the par value. While there are several reasons why bonds trade at premium, generally speaking, this occurs when the coupon rate on the bond is higher than the prevailing interest rate.

5. *Discount* is a way to say that the current price of the bond is less than the par value. There are quite a few reasons why a bond may trade at a discount, including current interest rate and speculation about the creditworthiness of the issuer.

6. The *conversion ratio* is the formula to determine how many shares of common stock a holder of a convertible bond could receive were they to choose to convert to stock. Here is the formula:

$$\frac{\text{par value of convertible bond}}{\text{conversion price of equity}}$$

CURRENT YIELD, YIELD TO CALL, YIELD TO MATURITY, YIELD TO WORST, AND BOND EQUIVALENT YIELD

1. *Current yield* illustrates the rate of return an investor would receive were he or she to purchase the bond today and hold it for one year. Here is the formula:

$$\frac{\text{annual income}}{\text{current price}}$$

2. *Yield to call* allows the holder of a bond to calculate the yield of a bond from date of purchase until date of call. It is calculated by determining the interest rate investors would receive were they to invest all coupon payments at a constant interest rate until the bond's call date.

3. *Yield to maturity* works the same way as yield to call except that the calculation takes into consideration all of the coupon payments until the bond's maturity date.

4. *Yield to worst* is the lowest yield that a bondholder could receive without the issuer of the debt defaulting. The calculation takes into consideration a few worst-case scenarios based on the underlying provisions of the bond in question.

5. Bond equivalent yield is used when bonds make coupon payments more frequently than annually. It enables investors to make fair comparisons between two bonds that have different payment streams.

Here is the formula:

$$\frac{\text{par value} - \text{purchase price}}{\text{purchase price}} \times \frac{365}{\text{days to maturity}}$$

TREASURY BILL, TREASURY NOTE, TREASURY BOND, AND MUNICIPAL BOND

1. A *treasury bill* is a U.S. government security with a maturity of less than one year.
2. A *treasury note* is a U.S. government security with a maturity of more than one year but less than 10 years.
3. A *treasury bond* is a U.S. government security with a maturity of more than 10 years.
4. A *municipal bond* is a security issued by a city or locality. These are also called *tax-exempt securities* because they are exempt from federal taxation.

TYPES OF AGENCY SECURITIES

An *agency security* is a debt that is issued by one of the U.S. government-sponsored entities (GSEs). Examples of these include the Student Loan Marketing Association (SLMA), Federal National Mortgage Association (FNMA), and the Federal Home Loan Bank. Each state has different rules about whether the interest earned from these securities is taxable.

CAPITAL RESTRUCTURING, SHARE REPURCHASE PROGRAM AND TENDER OFFER

1. A *capital restructuring* is a change in how the company finances its operations. A company that previously used corporate bonds as its primary source of capital may choose to retire some of the debt and instead introduce an initial public offering (IPO) on the primary market.
2. A *share repurchase program* is when a company buys back some of its own shares, thereby decreasing the number of shares that remain outstanding. This is often initiated by companies that believe their shares are significantly undervalued.
3. A *tender offer* occurs when a company offers to buy back some or all of its shares at a premium to what the shares are trading at in the market.

REGISTRATION STATEMENT AND PROXY STATEMENT

A *registration statement* is a set of documents that a company is required to file with the Securities & Exchange Commission (SEC) before going forward with its initial public offering (IPO). It includes the prospectus, financial statements, and general information about how the company intends to utilize the proceeds from the offering. A *proxy statement* is a document that a company files with the SEC that provides information that will be discussed at an upcoming stockholder meeting, including executive compensation and board of director elections.

THREE UNLAWFUL PRACTICES REFERENCED IN SECURITIES EXCHANGE ACT (SEA) RULE 13E-3 (PRIVATE TRANSACTIONS)

The three unlawful practices referenced in Securities Exchange Act (SEA) Rule 13e-3 are these:

1. Implementing any scheme or utilizing any device with the intention of defrauding an investor
2. Making statements about securities that are not truthful or leaving out material information that would affect an investor's decision
3. Engaging in any fraudulent practices during the course of business or participating in any act that would cause deceit

FOUR DISCLOSURES THAT PRIVATE ISSUERS MUST MAKE TO INVESTORS

The four disclosures required under Securities Exchange Act (SEA) Rule 13e-3 are these:

1. A completed summary term sheet
2. A special factors section that is prominently displayed
3. A legend on the front cover that indicates that the Securities & Exchange Commission (SEC) has not confirmed the accuracy of the information
4. An appraisal rights disclosure

INFORMATION REQUIRED TO BE INCLUDED IN A TENDER OFFER

A tender offer is not complete unless it contains all of the following information:

1. The number of shares the company wants to repurchase
2. The names of those from whom the company will repurchase shares
3. The exchange or quotation system on which the shares will be repurchased
4. The distinct purpose for the repurchase
5. Whether the company will dispose of the securities or hold them in its treasury
6. Whether the company is borrowing the funds to make the repurchase or if they are using company funds to implement the tender offer

JOINT TENANTS WITH RIGHTS OF SURVIVORSHIP (JTWROS) AND JOINT TENANTS IN COMMON (JTIC)

Joint tenants with rights of survivorship (JTWROS) is a type of account where at least two people are owners and they all have equal rights to the account's assets. Upon the death of one of the owners, the ownership passes to the remaining surviving tenants. *Joint tenants in common (JTIC)* is a type of account where at least two people are owners; however, at death, each owner has the right to designate his or her portion of the account assets to his or her estate.

GROWTH AT A REASONABLE PRICE (GARP), GROWTH, AGGRESSIVE GROWTH, AND CAPITAL APPRECIATION

1. *Growth at a reasonable price (GARP)* is an investment strategy that looks to combine growth investing and value investment strategies. A GARP investor is one who tries to find companies that are showing consistent earnings growth while not considering those that have very high valuations. The underlying goal is to eliminate the risks involved with purchasing only growth assets or value assets.
2. A *growth* company is one that generates positive cash flows that tend to increase at a faster rate than the overall economy. These companies tend to have high retained earnings. Rather than paying dividends, it focuses the profits on expanding the business and producing higher long-term returns.
3. The term *aggressive growth* is generally associated with mutual funds. It signifies that the fund is looking to achieve the highest capital gains possible and often has larger price swings due to the volatility of the underlying stocks.
4. *Capital appreciation* is simply the rise in the value of an asset due to the increase in market price. Many mutual funds have this as a stated investment goal. In these funds, the managers try to purchase investments that will rise in value due to increased earnings (rather than dividend or interest income inflating the returns).

DISTRESSED ASSETS, VALUE STOCK AND MOMENTUM TRADING

1. *Distressed assets* are those that are nearing (or are even in the process of) bankruptcy. They are securities that are unable to meet their obligations, and as a result, their investment value has fallen.
2. A *value stock* is one that trades at a price that is lower than its fundamentals indicate it should. These stocks are considered undervalued, and as such, investors believe that they have potential to increase in price. These stocks often have a high dividend yield and low price-to-earnings ratios.
3. *Momentum trading* is a strategy that looks to take advantage of the existing trends in the market. An investor using this strategy believes that large increases in prices will be followed by additional gains and large decreases will be followed by additional losses. This type of investor often does not predict trends so much as jumps on the band wagon once the market begins to move.

ARBITRAGE AND QUANTITATIVE TRADING

1. *Arbitrage* occurs when an investor is able to profit from a difference in the price of an asset. This profit occurs due to market inefficiencies but is harder to take advantage of with advancements in technology.
2. *Quantitative trading* looks at the underlying mathematical analyses to determine trading opportunities. This type of strategy is often utilized by extremely sophisticated investors as well as by hedge funds and financial institutions. It can be characterized by trades that are large in size and quick turnover to take advantage of short-term market movements.

TYPES OF RISKS FACED BY INVESTORS

The main types of risks faced by investors are these:

1. *Interest rate risk:* This is the risk that a debt security will decline in value due to a rise in interest rates.
2. *Market risk:* This is also known as *systematic risk*. It is the risk that all of your assets will lose value in the same manner.
3. *Business risk:* This is also known as *unsystematic risk*. It is the risk that a particular company within an industry will not see the same investment return as its competitors.
4. *Credit risk*: This is the risk that a bondholder will not be able to make all of its interest and principal payments.
5. *Inflationary risk:* This is the risk that the value of an asset will be eroded due to inflation. In other words, the investor does not have as much purchasing power.
6. *Liquidity risk:* This is the risk that an investor will be unable to sell a security at a moment's notice.
7. *Reinvestment risk:* This is the risk that, when a bond matures, the investor will be unable to use the proceeds to purchase a bond with equal or greater interest rates.

C CORPORATION, S CORPORATION AND LIMITED LIABILITY COMPANY

1. *C corporations* are businesses that are legally organized in order to limit their owner's financial and legal liabilities. These entities are taxed at a corporate level. Taxation at a personal level occurs only when there are distributions of income or capital.
2. *S corporations* are an option when a corporation has fewer than 10 shareholders. It provides the benefit of limited liability; however, the profits are not taxed at the corporate level but rather on the shareholders' personal tax returns.
3. A *limited liability company* is a legal entity where partners of the company are not held personally responsible for the company's liabilities. The taxation in this type of entity flows through to the partners' tax returns.

TRUST, MASTER LIMITED PARTNERSHIP (MLP), REAL ESTATE INVESTMENT TRUST (REIT), AND HEDGE FUND

1. A *trust* is a legal entity in which one party (the grantor or trustor) gives future rights to designated property or assets to other people (the beneficiaries). The trust is administered by a third party (the trustee). Trusts can be revocable (where the grantor is still alive and is permitted to be the trustee), irrevocable (where the grantor is still alive but is not permitted to be the trustee), or testamentary (where the grantor is deceased).
2. A *master limited partnership (MLP)* is a publicly traded security that derives at least 90 percent of its cash flows from real estate, natural resources, and commodities. It is run by a general partner and receives capital from investors who are considered the limited partners.
3. A *real estate investment trust (REIT)* is a security that invests in real estate by either purchasing properties or mortgages.
4. A hedge fund is a limited partnership that is considered a sophisticated strategy and often involves larger initial capital investment. A hedge fund uses high-risk methods to attempt to realize large capital gains.

ACCREDITED INVESTOR AND VENTURE CAPITAL

1. An *accredited investor* is an individual who makes at least $200,000 per year (or $300,000 with a spouse) or has a net worth of at least $1 million.
2. *Venture capital* is the money provided by investors to help start-up firms. This is a way for small businesses that do not have access to the capital markets to get the money they need without utilizing bank loans as their sole source of funding.

BUY-SIDE AND SELL-SIDE TRANSACTIONS

Buy-side is considered the Wall Street side of the financial industry. It is made up of the institutions that purchase securities for money-management purposes and investors who buy for their own accounts. *Sell-side* is the investment banking and research analysis side of the financial industry. This is the side of the business that creates new securities and makes recommendations about both new and existing securities.

QUALIFIED INSTITUTIONAL BUYER

A qualified institutional buyer is one of the following:

1. An insurance company, including one that purchases the security for a separate account
2. An investment company
3. A business development company
4. A small business investment company
5. A state plan, including ones for political subdivisions
6. An employee benefit plan
7. A trust fund whose trustee is a bank or trust company
8. A 501C3. charitable organization
9. An investment advisor
10. A dealer registered under Section 15 of the Exchange Act, purchasing for his or her own account or for the account of another qualified institutional buyer
11. A dealer registered under Section 15 of the Exchange Ac purchasing as part of a riskless transaction for the account of another qualified institutional buyer
12. Any entity in which all of the owners are qualified institutional buyers
13. Any bank, savings, and loan associations that invest at least $100 million in securities with which it is not affiliated and have a value of at least $25 million according to their most recent financial statements

REASONABLE GROUND FOR BELIEF UNDER THE SECURITIES EXCHANGE ACT (SEA) RULE 176

The factors that should be considered when deciding whether an individual who signed a registration statement had reasonable ground for believe include the following:

1. The type of issuer
2. The type of security
3. The type of person
4. If the person was an officer and the office held
5. If the person was a director and the presence or absence of another relationship to the issuer
6. If the person was an underwriter, the type of arrangement, the role of the particular person, and the availability of information

33

7. To what degree the person relied on officers, employees, and others to give him or her knowledge of particular facts
8. Whether the particular person had any responsibility over the facts in the document at the time it was filed

COMMISSION'S REVIEW DISCLOSURES MADE BY ISSUERS UNDER THE SARBANES-OXLEY ACT

To be in compliance with the Sarbanes-Oxley Act, the Commission will review disclosures made by issuers for the protection of investors. This includes a review of the issuer's financial statements. When determining the order in which to schedule these reviews, the Commission will consider the following factors:

1. The extent to which issuers have issued material restatements of financial results
2. The extent to which issuers experience volatility as compared to others
3. Issuers with the largest market capitalization
4. Emerging companies with disparities in price-to-earnings ratios
5. Issuers whose operations materially impact any other sector of the economy

PERSONAL LOAN TO EXECUTIVE'S CONFLICT OF INTEREST RULE

In general, issuers may not make personal loans to executives. However, if a loan was made prior to the enactment of Sarbanes-Oxley Act, it is permitted to stay on the books so long as the loan is not renewed or modified. Personal loans do not include those that are made in the ordinary course of business.

DISCLOSURE REQUIREMENTS OF ANY DIRECTOR, OFFICER, OR PRINCIPAL STOCKHOLDER OF A PUBLICLY TRADED COMPANY

Anyone who owns more than 10 percent of a class of a security or is a director or an officer of a publicly traded company is required to file a statement as to his or her ownership each time he or she makes purchases or sales of company stock. The statement filed should include the date of purchase or sale, the number of shares, the price at which the shares were purchased or sold, as well as any other pertinent details. This statement is then processed through the electronic data gathering, analysis, and retrieval (EDGAR) system.

CREATING AND ASSESSING INTERNAL CONTROLS FOR FINANCIAL REPORTING

Each year, the management of a publicly traded company must submit a report indicating its responsibility for establishing and maintaining adequate procedures for financial reporting as well as an assessment as to how effective current procedures are. In addition, each public accounting firm that prepares audit reports for an issuer must attest to the assessment made by the management team.

Underwriting/New Financing Transactions, Types of Offerings, and Registration of Securities

Offering Document and Road Show Presentation

1. An *offering document* is a legal document that includes the objectives, terms, and underlying risks of a new issue. It includes additional information that investors would want to see to determine their interest, including financial statements, information about the management team, and a detailed description of the business.
2. A *road show presentation* is a presentation made by an issuer to potential buyers. The team travels around the country and gives presentations to analysts, fund managers, and individual wealthy investors.

Prefiling Period Rules

The *prefiling period* refers to the time in between when the company reaches an agreement with the managing underwriters to the time when the company files the registration statement with the Securities & Exchange Commission (SEC). The company is not allowed to make any offers to sell during this time period, even if it has a prospectus to accompany the offer. Because the SEC realizes that the issuer cannot forego all forms of advertising during this time period, there is a list of rules that should be followed:

1. The disclosure is consistent with the issuer's prior practice.
2. The disclosure is in customary form.
3. The disclosure does not contain projections, forecasts, predictions, opinions, or valuations.
4. The content, timing, and distribution of the disclosure does not suggest that a selling effort is underway.

Financial Industry Regulatory Authority (FINRA) Mediation Process

Mediation is considered a more informal process than arbitration. A mediator does not issue a decision but rather is brought in to help guide the parties involved to a joint resolution. The process tends to look like this:

1. The parties file a request to mediate form to begin the process.
2. A mediator is selected.
3. Mediation sessions are scheduled and take place—often multiple sessions are required.
4. A *settlement* is said to occur when parties resolve their dispute. An *impasse* is said to occur when the parties are unable to resolve their dispute and another means of resolving the dispute will be taken.

Filing of Emerging-Growth Company Registration Statements Exceptions

For the most part, emerging-growth companies have the same requirements for their registration statements. However, emerging-growth companies only need to present two years of audited financial statements to be in compliance with the Commission. In addition, they do not need to present the selected financial data required of other companies.

REGISTRATION STATEMENT

Thirty-two main sections:

1. Description of business
2. Description of property
3. Legal proceedings
4. Mine safety disclosure (if applicable)
5. Market price and dividends
6. Description of the security
7. Financial data for last five fiscal years
8. Supplemental financial information (net sales, profit, per share values, and net income)
9. Management's financial analysis on the condition of the company's operations
10. Accountants or accounting changes in the last two fiscal years
11. Market risk disclosure (both quantitative and qualitative analysis)
12. Controls or procedures for executives and officers
13. Controls for financial reporting
14. Specific holdings of management and key stockholders
15. List of directors, officers, and control persons
16. Executive compensation (including directors)
17. Transactions for officers, directors, and control persons over the last fiscal year
18. Company's code of ethics
19. Corporate governance
20. Outside front cover page of prospectus
21. Inside front and outside back cover pages of prospectus
22. Summary of prospectus and risk factors
23. Use of proceeds from offering
24. How the offering price was determined
25. Dilution
26. Selling security holders
27. Distribution plan
28. Interests for any named experts and legal counsel
29. Commission disclosure
30. Expenses incurred during issuance and distribution
31. Undertakings
32. Exhibits referenced in any of the sections

SMALLER COMPANY REQUIREMENT

The only 12 sections that a smaller reporting company is required to include are these:

1. Description of business
2. Market price and dividends
3. Financial data for the last five fiscal years
4. Supplemental financial information (net sales, profit, per share values, and net income)
5. Management's financial analysis on the condition of the company's operations
6. Market risk disclosure (both quantitative and qualitative analysis)
7. Executive compensation (including directors)
8. Transactions for officers, directors, and control persons over the last fiscal year
9. Corporate governance

10. Summary of prospectus and risk factors
11. Use of proceeds from offering
12. Exhibits referenced in any of the sections

SECURITIES EXCHANGE ACT (SEA) REGULATION S-X

Requirements for filing financial statements:

1. The accountants preparing the financial statements must be qualified to do so.
2. The accountants must file an attestation report.
3. The financial statements must be reviewed by foreign government auditors (if applicable).
4. The financial statements must be reviewed by someone who is not affiliated with the company.
5. The financial statements must be reviewed by more than one person.
6. The audit and review records must be retained for a period of at least seven years.
7. All communication with audit committees must be documented.
8. A consolidated balance sheet must be filed.
9. A consolidated statement of income and changes in financial position must be filed.
10. A report showing changes in stockholders' equity must be filed.
11. Financial statements for any businesses acquired (or soon to be acquired) must be filed.
12. Financial statements for the last 9 to 12 months must be readily available.
13. Separate financial statements for any subsidiary companies must be filed.
14. Separate financial statements for any guarantors for a guaranteed security must be filed.

FORM S-1, FORM S-3, FORM S-4, AND FORM S-8

1. Form S-1 is used when a company is planning a public offering. The form includes information such as: business model, competitors, how the price was determined, and details of the plans for the proceeds from the offering.
2. Form S-3 is similar to the S-1, but it is a simplified version that companies may use if they meet the reporting requirements referenced in Section 12 or 15(d) of the Securities Act of 1934.
3. Form S-4 is used in the event of a merger or acquisition. It is a compilation of disclosures and pertinent details that investors need in order to determine whether to buy, hold, or sell shares.
4. Form S-8 is used in the event that company stock is or will be an available option in certain employee benefit plans.

DIVIDEND REINVESTMENT PLAN (DRIP)

A *dividend reinvestment plan (DRIP)* is one that allows investors to automatically take the dividends paid out by a company and purchase more shares directly from treasury stock. While there is not a tax incentive available for participating in this type of arrangement, in many cases, the company sponsoring the plan will offer a small discount on the purchase price of the shares.

Foreign Private Issuer

A *foreign private issuer* is any foreign issuer other than a foreign government. There are exceptions to this definition. The exceptions include any issuer that meets the following criteria as of the end of the most recent fiscal quarter:

1. More than 50 percent of the outstanding voting shares are owned by residents of the United States in addition to one of the following:
   a. A majority of the directors or company officers are citizens or residents of the United States.
   b. The business is operated for the most part in the United States.

Promoter, Shell Company, Significant Subsidiary, and Smaller Reporting Company

1. A *promoter* is any person or company that helps raise investment capital for a fee. Generally, these investments are not traditional in nature.
2. A *shell company* is one where there are no assets held within the company, nor do business operations take place under the name of the company. Start-up firms often legitimately use this structure; however, in other cases, it can be a sign of illegal activities.
3. A *significant subsidiary* is one that makes up more than 10 percent of the total assets of the parent company or more than 10 percent of the income earned by the parent company.
4. A *smaller reporting company* is a term that the Securities & Exchange Commission (SEC) uses to indicate that a company is not required to file as complex of forms and reports as its larger counterparts due to its size. In general, a smaller reporting company will have annual revenue less than $50 million.

Well-Known Seasoned Issuer, Seasoned Issuer and Unseasoned Issuer

1. A *well-known seasoned issuer* is one that has filed its reports in a timely fashion for the past year and has more than $700 million of common equity public float or has issued at least $1 billion in nonconvertible debt or preferred stock during the prior three-year time period.
2. A *seasoned issuer* is one that has filed its reports in a timely fashion for the past year but does not meet the equity criteria to be categorized as a well-known seasoned issuer.
3. An *unseasoned issuer* is one that has not been current with its filings at some point during the past year.

Continuous Basis or on a Delayed Basis Security Registration

For the registration of a security to be made on a continuous basis or on a delayed basis, the registration statement may only pertain to the following:

1. Securities that will be offered to or sold by individuals other than the registrant or a subsidiary of the registrant
2. Securities in dividend reinvestment plans (DRIPs) or employee benefit plans
3. Securities that will be issued due to the exercise of options, rights, or warrants already outstanding
4. Securities that are pledged as collateral
5. Mortgage securities, including mortgage-backed debt
6. Securities issued in relation with business transactions
7. Securities issued on Form S-3 or F-6
8. Securities that will be offered through a closed-end management investment company or a business development company

AUTOMATIC SHELF REGISTRATION STATEMENT

An *automatic shelf registration statement,* also known as *Securities & Exchange Commission (SEC) Rule 415,* allows companies to meet the filing requirements with the SEC up to three years before an offering is officially available to the public. During the time between filing this statement and the time of offering, the company is still required to file all quarterly and annual statements.

SECURITIES EXCHANGE ACT (SEA) SECTION 10A

AUDIT OF FINANCIAL STATEMENTS

When auditing financial statements, there must be procedures in place that are designed to accomplish the following:

1. Identify illegal acts that materially impact the financial statements
2. Identify related-party transactions that require additional disclosures
3. Identify the likelihood of whether the company will be continue to be in business the following year

ILLEGAL ACTS

If during the course of an audit, the auditor determines that illegal acts have occurred, the auditor is required to immediately notify the audit committee. If after making this disclosure, the auditor determines that the audit committee has not sufficiently remedied the situation, then the auditor will bring his or her concerns to the attention of the board of directors. If the board of directors does not take immediate action, then the auditor will provide a copy of the report to the Commission.

PROSPECTUS AND FREE WRITING PROSPECTUS

1. A *prospectus* is a legal document that provides details about an offering that is being made to the public, including information about the stocks (or bonds) themselves as well as the operations of the business. A prospectus can be either in preliminary or final form. Because the letters on the front are printed in red, this document can also be known as a red herring.
2. A *free writing prospectus* is a supplemental document that accompanies the formal prospectus, which details additional information about the business or the actual offering. It is still required to be reviewed by the Securities & Exchange Commission (SEC) and must contain a legend.

NUMBER OF COPIES OF THE PROSPECTUS TO BE FILED

An issuer is required to submit five copies of any prospectus that is given to any potential investor prior to the effective registration statement date. In certain situations, ten copies are required. Those situations include the following:

1. A prospectus that corrects information released in a previous version of the prospectus
2. A prospectus that provides information omitted in a previous version of the prospectus
3. A prospectus in connection with a security being issued on a delayed basis
4. A prospectus in connection with a security subject to Canada's National Policy Statement Number 45

FILING A PROSPECTUS

In general, a prospectus must require all information pertaining to an offering. However, if all of the following criteria are met, a prospectus can be filed before all information is known or readily available (rather than delaying the filing):

1. The initial offering transaction was completed prior to the filing.
2. Issuance of the securities occurred prior to the filing.
3. The registration statement uses generic terms to refer to any unnamed selling security holders.
4. In the prior three years, the issuer (including any predecessor) was not a blank-check company, a shell company, or an issuer of a penny stock offering

PERMISSIBLE TYPES OF COMMUNICATIONS THAT CAN BE MADE AHEAD OF THE FILING OF A REGISTRATION STATEMENT

According to Rule 163A of the Securities Act, communications that occur at least 30 days prior to a company filing a registration statement are permissible so long as the communication meets the following conditions:

1. It does not refer to the securities offering.
2. It is both authorized and made by the issuer.
3. The issuer takes reasonable steps to ensure that the communication is not distributed once the filing of the registration statement is within the 30-day time frame.

ORAL AND WRITTEN OFFERS MADE PRIOR TO THE FILING OF A REGISTRATION STATEMENT

Well-seasoned known issuers have substantially more freedoms than other issuers. They are free to make unrestricted oral and written offers so long as all of the following criteria are met:

1. The offering contains a legend.
2. The offering is filed with the Securities & Exchange Commission (SEC) at the time the registration statement is filed.
3. The offering is not related to any ineligible offerings (business combination transactions, issuers that are investment companies, or business development companies).

INFORMATION THAT AN ISSUER MAY COMMUNICATE THAT DO NOT MEET THE DEFINITION OF A PROSPECTUS

An issuer may communicate the following types of information without fearing that they are violating rules related to a prospectus:

- Publicly available factual information such as contact information for the business
- The name of the security and whether it will be convertible, exercisable, or exchangeable, including the ticker and Committee on Uniform Securities Identification Procedures (CUSIP).
- General information such as the principal products manufactured or services rendered by the company
- The price of the security or the way in which the price will be determined
- The interest rate for a fixed income security or the way in which the interest rate will be determined
- A brief description about the way in which the company will use the proceeds from the offering (so long as this statement is consistent with what is filed in the actual prospectus)
- The names of the underwriters

- The anticipated date on which the securities will be available to the public
- The dates, times, and locations of any upcoming marketing events
- Whether the security is exempt from any specific taxes, based on the opinion of the issuer's general counsel
- Any information necessary to correct an inaccurate statement made in accordance with one of the above items.

GENERIC ADVERTISEMENT

A *generic advertisement* is one that is limited to containing only the following information:

1. General information about the nature of or services offered by investment companies
2. General information about the various types of investment objectives (balanced funds, growth funds, or bond funds for example)
3. General descriptions of a product or service offered (but not specific enough to be applied to a certain security)
4. Invitation to inquire about additional information

FACTUAL BUSINESS INFORMATION

The term *factual business information* constitutes basic information about the company's business or financial developments, including dividend notices. It also includes advertisements about the company's products and services. To meet the definition, the following criteria must be met:

1. The information contained within the communication was disseminated previously.
2. The way in which the information is released (including timing, manner, and form) is consistent with the way in which it was disseminated previously.
3. The information is disseminated to the same class of individuals who have historically received it (e.g., customers and suppliers meet this classification; potential investors do not).
4. The issuing company is not registered under the Investment Company Act of 1940.
5. The issuing company is not a business development company.

TYPE OF REPORTS THAT DO NOT CONSTITUTE AN OFFER TO SELL A SECURITY

A broker–dealer may distribute the following types of reports for securities that he or she distributes without being deemed to have made an offer:

1. Issuer-specific research reports, so long as the broker–dealer distributes the reports on a regular basis, and therefore, the issuance of one is in keeping with general business practices and the following criteria are met:
   a. Minimum flat provisions are met, or the issuer is a well-known seasoned issuer.
   b. During the previous 12 months, all annual and quarterly filings were made on time.
   c. During the prior three years, the issuer was not a blank-check company, a shell company, or the issuer of a penny stock.
2. Industry reports, so long as the broker–dealer distributes the reports on a regular basis, and therefore, the issuance of one is in keeping with general business practices and the following criteria are met:
   a. The report includes information about a substantial number of issuers in that particular industry.
   b. The analysis does not spotlight one particular issuer (either through word choice or amount of space given in the write-up).

REGISTRATION STATEMENT LAWSUIT

In the event that a registration statement contains an untrue statement of material information or omits key information, the following individuals may be held liable by a purchaser of the security:

1. Anyone who signed the registration statement
2. Anyone who was on the board of directors at the time the registration statement was filed
3. Anyone who is named in the registration statement as about to become a director with the company
4. Anyone who was involved in the preparation of the registration statement, including accountants and appraisers
5. The underwriter of the security

DAMAGES RECOUPED THROUGH A LAWSUIT

The damages the investor may attempt to recoup through the filing of a lawsuit include one of the following:

1. The price at which the security was offered to the public
2. The price at which the security would have been disposed of in the market prior to the filing of the lawsuit
3. The lesser of the price at which the security would have been disposed of in the market at the time of judgment or the difference between the amount paid for the security and the value of the security at the time of the filing of the lawsuit
4. In addition, at the discretion of the judge, the reasonable attorney fees and court costs paid by the investor

MAKING OFFERS OR SALES OF SECURITIES THROUGH THE MAIL

It is unlawful to use the mail system to make an offer to sell securities to do the following:

1. Defraud an investor
2. Obtain money by making untrue statements of material importance or omitting key information
3. Use a business practice to deceive a purchaser
4. Advertise the offering of a security without fully disclosing the amount of monetary consideration that has been received from an underwriter, issuer, or dealer
5. State that the fact that a registration statement has been received by the Securities & Exchange Commission (SEC) is in any way an indication that the registration statement is accurate and complete

FORWARD-LOOKING STATEMENT

A *forward-looking statement* is one that contains any of the following information:

1. Projection of any financial items, including dividends, capital expenditures, revenues, income or losses, or earnings per share
2. Management's plans and objectives for future business operations
3. Future performance from management's discussion of financial condition of the company or analysis of operations

SEC Requirements to Protect Investors or Upheld Public Interest

The pieces of information that the Securities & Exchange Commission (SEC) may require an issuer to provide are these:

1. Organizational chart, financial structuring, and general nature of the business
2. Terms, rights, and privileges of the different classes of outstanding securities
3. Terms for the offered or outstanding securities during the previous three years
4. List of any director, officer, underwriter, or other investor holding more than 10 percent of outstanding shares, along with any material contracts or other interests that exist between each individual and the issuer
5. Payment made to anyone who is not an officer or director if such amount exceeds $20,000 per year
6. Bonus and profit-sharing plan information
7. Management employee contracts
8. Options currently in place or those to be created in the near future
9. Material contracts that are not considered to be part of ordinary course of business that will be executed (fully or partially) at or after the filing of the application
10. Balance sheets for the prior three fiscal years certified by a public accounting firm
11. Profit and loss statements for the prior three fiscal years certified by a public accounting firm
12. Any other financial statements that the SEC believes are necessary to protect investors
13. Copies of articles of incorporation, trust indentures, or other documents that the SEC believes are necessary to protect investors

Unlisted Trading Privileges

A national securities exchange may extend unlisted trading privileges to the following:

1. A security that is listed and registered on a national securities exchange
2. A security that is otherwise registered or would be were they not exempt from the registration requirements

Suspension of Unlisted Trading Privileges

The Commission will not permit (or will suspend) unlisted trading privileges in the following scenarios:

1. Extending unlisted trading privileges would not allow for the markets to remain fair and orderly.
2. Extending unlisted trading privileges would negatively impact the existing market for such a security.
3. Extending unlisted trading privileges would impair dealers to effectuate transactions in the security for their own accounts or between dealers acting as market makers.

Reinstatement of a Security's Unlisted Trading Privileges

In the event that a national security exchange wishes to extend unlisted trading privileges to a security where the Commission previously denied or suspended the extension, the following steps must be taken:

1. The exchange will file an application with the Commission.
2. The Commission will set up a hearing to review the request within 10 days of the filing.

3. If the Commission finds that the reason the request was denied previously has been resolved and no new hindrances are in place, the Commission will approve the request. Otherwise, the request will be denied, and the exchange will not be allowed to extend the privilege.

REQUIRED SECURITIES TO FILE A REGISTRATION STATEMENT

Describe the securities that are required to file a registration statement with the Commission in accordance with the interstate commerce rules of Section 12(g).

INVESTOR'S PROTECTION

In the event of an emergency, the Commission may take action to alter, supplement, suspend, or impose requirements to accomplish the following:

1. Restore fair and orderly markets.
2. Assure accurate clearance and settlement of trades.
3. Reduce or eliminate substantial disruption in the markets, including a segment of one.
4. Ensure appropriate processing of securities transactions.

EMERGENCY

The term *emergency* refers to a significant disturbance in one of the following ways:

1. Sudden and extreme fluctuations in prices (or the significant threat of it)
2. Disruption in the clearing and settling of transactions (or the significant threat of it)
3. Disruption in the processing of securities transactions (or the significant threat of it)

DISCLOSURE OF NONPUBLIC INFORMATION

An issuer is not required to publicly disclose material, nonpublic information that was shared with a specific person in the following situations:

1. The person receiving the information is in a position of confidence were a duty of trust exists (e.g., an attorney).
2. The person receiving the information is covered by a nondisclosure agreement.
3. The information is disclosed in a registration statement.
4. The information is disclosed in a free writing prospectus.

ENTERING INTO CONTRACT WITH AN ISSUER

When a member enters into contract with an issuer, the member is required to disclose to customers that the relationship exists as well as any compensation arrangement that may exist. If the disclosure is given to customers orally, then it must be followed up as a supplemental disclosure at or before the completion of the first transaction related to any security of that issuer.

DELIVERING A PROSPECTUS

A dealer is not obligated to deliver a prospectus in the following scenarios:

1. The registration statement is on a Form F-6 (ADR-registration form).
2. Prior to the filing of the registration statement, the issuer was subject to Section 13 or 15d of the Securities Exchange Act of 1934.
3. The registration statement relates to an offering that is made from time to time, and the initial prospectus was already delivered.

NUMBER OF COPIES OF A PRELIMINARY PROSPECTUS

The Commission does not provide a specific number of preliminary prospectus copies that an issuer should make available. Rather, it indicates that the issuer should have enough copies made to accommodate the following:

1. Ensure that each underwriter and dealer who is reasonably expected to participate in the distribution has access to the preliminary prospectus.
2. Ensure that the preliminary prospectus is made available to any closed-end investment company that is involved in the distribution

DISTRIBUTING PRELIMINARY PROSPECTUSES TO CUSTOMERS

A broker–dealer is required to distribute a preliminary prospectus in accordance with the following rules:

1. Any person who will receive a confirmation of sale must receive the preliminary prospectus at least 48 hours prior to sending the confirmation.
2. Any person who requests the preliminary prospectus between the filing date and the effective date of the registration statement (or a reasonable time before this date) should receive a copy of the latest preliminary prospectus.
3. The broker–dealer needs to provide copies of the latest preliminary prospectus to anyone associated with the practice who will be soliciting customer orders.
4. If the broker–dealer is the managing underwriter, then all broker–dealers associated with the distribution should receive copies of the latest preliminary prospectus.

REGISTRATION FILINGS

An issuer is required to submit to the Securities & Exchange Commission (SEC) the following registration documents:

1. Three copies of the registration statement (including the offering circular, offering memorandum, notification of filing, notice of intention, application for conversion, and any other document that may be used to offer securities)
2. Three copies of any proposed underwriting agreements (including the agreement among underwriters, selected dealers agreement, agency agreement, purchase agreement, letter of intent, consulting agreement, partnership agreement, underwriter's warrant agreement, escrow agreement, and any other document that describes the arrangements for the underwriting and distribution of the securities)
3. Three copies of each amendment to the registration statement (one copy marked to show changes)
4. Three copies of the final registration statement that is declared effective by the SEC
5. One copy of any document that is filed with the SEC through the electronic data gathering, analysis, and retrieval (EDGAR) system

INFORMATION REQUIRED BY FINRA

The specific information that the Financial Industry Regulatory Authority (FINRA) requires be provided electronically includes the following:

1. An estimate of the maximum offering price
2. An estimate of the maximum underwriting discount or commission
3. An estimate of the maximum reimbursement of the underwriter's expenses and counsel's fees

4. An estimate of the maximum financial consulting or advisory fees to the underwriter
5. An estimate of the maximum finder's fees
6. A statement of any other compensation that may be payable to the underwriter
7. A statement indicating the relationship that may exist between an officer or director and anyone who owns 5 percent or more of the issuer's securities.
8. An explanation of any arrangement that became effective during the 180-day period leading up to the offering date that involves the transfer of any security to the underwriter or related person.

EXEMPTIONS FROM FILING

The five types of offerings that are exempt from filing with the Financial Industry Regulatory Authority (FINRA) include the following:

1. Securities (other than an initial public offering) issued by a foreign government or foreign government agency that has unsecured, nonconvertible debt with a maturity of at least four years with a nationally recognized rating that falls into the one of the four highest rating categories
2. Securities offered by a foreign private issuer or under the laws of Canada
3. Securities that are backed by financial instruments and are rated by a nationally recognized organization with a rating that falls into one of the four highest categories
4. Securities that will be issued or the securities that will be acquired are listed with the Nasdaq Global Market, New York Stock Exchange, or American Stock Exchange
5. Securities that are offered by a charitable organization that is exempt from Securities & Commission (SEC) registration

UNDERWRITING COMPENSATION

The following items are all considered to have value under the terminology of *underwriting compensation*:

1. Discount or Commission
2. Reimbursement of expenses
3. Fees and expenses for underwriter's counsel
4. Finder's fees
5. Wholesaler's fees
6. Financial consulting and advisory fees
7. Securities, including common or preferred stock, stock options, and warrants

EXEMPTIONS FROM THE TERM UNDERWRITING COMPENSATION

The following items do not count as *underwriting compensation*:

1. Blue sky and other registration fees, Financial Industry Regulatory Authority (FINRA) filing fees, and accountant's fees
2. Cash compensation paid for acting as a placement agent in a private placement arrangement or for providing a loan or other service in a merger or acquisition
3. Listed securities purchased in public market transactions
4. Employer securities benefits: stock bonuses, pensions, or profit-sharing plans
5. Securities acquired by a company registered under the Investment Company Act
6. Nonconvertible or non-exchangeable debt securities that are purchased at fair market value in an unrelated transaction
7. Derivative investments that are purchased at fair market value in an unrelated transaction

SECURITIES AS PART OF COMPENSATION

Should an underwriter (or anyone related to the underwriter) receive securities as part of compensation, there must be a known valuation. The value may either be determined based on the price of an identical security offered in an independent market or by using one of the valuation formulas specifically permitted.

FORMULA TO DETERMINE THE VALUATION OF SECURITIES

To determine the valuation of securities received as part of underwriting compensation where the shares do not have an exercise or conversion price, the following steps should be followed:

Step 1: Market price per share on the date of acquisition* – per share cost.

   *If the market price is not known, use the public offering price.

Step 2: Multiply the result of Step 1 by the number of shares received.

Step 3: Divide the result from Step 2 by the offering proceeds.

Step 4: Multiply the result from Step 3 by 100.

Step 5: If the lock-up period is 180 days or less, stop here.

Step 6: If the lock-up period exceeds 180 days, multiply the result from Step 4 by 90 percent (i.e., receive a 10 percent discount).

FORMULA TO DETERMINE THE VALUATION OF WARRANTS

To determine the valuation of warrants received as part of underwriting compensation where the shares have an exercise or conversion price, the following steps should be followed:

Step 1: Public offering price per share x 65 percent – exercise price – market price per share on date of acquisition.*

   *If the market price is not known, use the public offering price.

Step 2: Divide the result from Step 1 by 2.

Step 3: Multiply the result from Step 2 by the number of securities underlying the warrants.

Step 4: Subtract the result from Step 3 by the total price paid for the warrants.

Step 5: Divide the result from Step 4 by the offering proceeds.

Step 6: Multiply the result from Step 5 by 100.

Step 7: If the lock-up period is 180 days or less, stop here.

Step 8: If the lock-up period exceeds 180 days, multiply the result from Step 6 by 90 percent (i.e., receive a 10 percent discount).

12 PROHIBITED ARRANGEMENTS ASSOCIATED WITH UNDERWRITING COMPENSATION PACKAGES

The prohibited arrangements are the following:

1. Payment for any accountable expense that the underwriter would incur during the normal course of business (e.g., salaries or supplies)
2. Any non-accountable expense that exceeds more than 3 percent of the offering proceeds
3. Payment of any compensation prior to the public sale of the securities being offered except that which is reasonably expected to be incurred prior to the commencement of the offering
4. Any tail-fee arrangement that extends more than two years from the date the services are terminated
5. Any first right of refusal to provide the underwriter the opportunity to underwrite future public offerings that has a duration of more than three years from the commencement of the offering to the public or has more than one opportunity to waive the right of refusal in exchange for a payment.
6. Payment to terminate a first right of refusal that has a value greater than 1 percent of the offering proceeds in the offering where the right was granted or is not paid in cash
7. Compensation consists of options, warrants, or convertible security has one of these factors:
    a. Is exercisable or convertible more than five years after the date of the offering
    b. Has more than one demand registration right at the issuer's expense
    c. Has a demand registration right with a duration of more than five years
    d. Has a piggyback registration right with a duration of more than seven years
    e. Has antidilution terms that allow the underwriter to receive additional shares at a lower price than initially agreed upon or to receive or accrue cash dividends
8. Valuation of the compensation that cannot be determined at the time of the offering
9. In a firm commitment basis, any over allotment option allowing for more than 15 percent of the securities
10. Receipt of warrants, options, convertible securities, or units containing these securities along with the following:
    a. The market price is lower than the exercise or conversion price.
    b. The warrant, option, or convertible security is held in a discretionary account at the time of the exercise or conversion (unless the customer gives specific permission).
    c. The specific compensation arrangements associated with the warrant, option, or convertible security are not disclosed in the prospectus or offering circular.
    d. The exercise or conversion of the warrants, options, or convertible securities cannot be solicited by the underwriter.
11. For a member to participate with an issuer in the distribution of non-underwritten issue of securities if the issuer hired people specifically for that purpose
12. For a member to participate in a public offering of real estate investment trust securities unless the trustee discloses the information in each annual report

CONFLICT OF INTEREST

In the event that a member has a conflict of interest with a public offering, he or she may participate so long as that member is not primarily responsible nor affiliated with the individual who will be managing the public offering. There must be a prominent disclosure detailing the conflict of interest in the prospectus or offering circular. In addition, a qualified independent underwriter must participate in the preparation of the prospectus and any other registration documents.

CONFLICT OF INTEREST RELATED TO A MEMBER'S ABILITY TO PARTICIPATE IN A PUBLIC OFFERING

A member has a *conflict of interest* when any of the following circumstances exist:

1. The issuer is controlled by or is under common control with the member, where control equals beneficial ownership of 10 percent or more.
2. Five percent or more of the net offering proceeds will be used to reduce or retire a loan held by the member.
3. As a result of the public offering, the member will become an affiliate of the issuer.
4. As a result of the public offering, the member will become publicly owned by the issuer.
5. As a result of the public offering, the issuer will become a member or form a broker–dealer subsidiary.

SYNDICATE, FIRM COMMITMENT, COMPETITIVE BID, AND NEGOTIATED SALE

1. A *syndicate* is a group of professional entities that is formed to handle a large transaction. To complete the transaction would be near impossible for any one entity on its own, but by temporarily pooling resources, the transaction can be completed more efficiently and with fewer risks to any one underlying firm.
2. A *firm commitment* is one where the underwriter agrees to purchase all securities directly from the issuer and sell them to the public at a specific price. In doing so, the underwriter assumes 100 percent of the risk.
3. A *competitive bid* is a process in which a sealed bid is submitted to the issuer from an underwriter. The issuer then selects the underwriter with the most favorable price and contract terms.
4. A *negotiated sale* is a process where the issuer and a selected underwriter work out the details for a public offering.

ALL OR NONE, BEST EFFORTS, GREENSHOE OPTION, AND LOCK-UP AGREEMENT

1. *All or none* is exactly as it sounds. The entire offering must be sold, or else the offering will be cancelled.
2. *Best efforts* is an agreement whereupon the underwriter promises to sell as much as possible of an offering to the public.
3. A *greenshoe option* is one where the underwriter has the right to sell more shares than originally planned by the issuer. This is also known as an *overallotment option*.
4. A *lock-up agreement* is a contract between an underwriter and an issuer where specified individuals are not permitted to sell any shares for a certain period of time. The most common lock-up arrangement is 180 days. Because restricted individuals often hold a very large number of shares, the sale of which can cause large fluctuations in the market, this type of agreement helps protect the stability of the stock price during the first few months of trading.

SOLICITING BIDS

Because, in an all or none underwriting arrangement, the offering will be voided unless all shares are sold, customers must be told at the time they purchase the shares that it is possible that their money will be refunded to them at the end of the specified time period. The money that a customer transmits as consideration for the shares must be held in a separate bank account until the end of the offering period, at which point the shares are either issued or the money is returned to the customer.

PURCHASING A COVERED SECURITY DURING THE RESTRICTED PERIOD

The following are permitted during the restricted period:

1. Publication of a research report, including ones that offer an opinion
2. Odd-lot transactions, including tender offers
3. Exercise of options, warrants, rights, or other convertible securities
4. Unsolicited transactions
5. Basket transactions, where a basket is 20 or more securities and the covered security does not make up more than 5 percent of the value of the basket
6. De minimis transactions, where the purchase is less than 2 percent of the average daily trading volume
7. Transactions related with a distribution that are not effected on an exchange, a quotation system, or an electronic communications network
8. Offers to sell the securities being distributed
9. Transactions eligible for resale under Rule 144A to qualified institutional buyers or individuals who are not U.S. persons.

BLUE SKY LAWS

Blue sky laws are state regulations that were put in place to protect investors against fraud involving securities. The laws require sellers to register their offerings and provide certain financial information. Doing so gives investors the information they need to judge the appropriateness of an offering. Every state has its own set of laws, but most of them come from the Uniform Securities Act of 1956. While no two states' wording is the same, in general, they all have language prohibiting sales agents from making unrealistic claims about the investment return or ignoring the underlying risks of the investment.

NATIONAL SECURITIES MARKET IMPROVEMENT ACT OF 1996

Because each state adopted its own set of blue sky laws, Congress passed the National Securities Market Improvement Act of 1966 to provide a uniform code that companies and regulators could use. One of the main provisions is to define the term *covered security*, which includes the following:

1. Nationally traded securities (i.e., listed securities on the New York Stock Exchange or American Stock Exchange or listed on the National Market System of the Nasdaq Stock Market)
2. Securities of a company registered under the Investment Company Act of 1940
3. Sales to qualified purchasers
4. Sales of certain exempt offerings

PUBLIC APPEARANCE

The term *public appearance* includes participation in a seminar, forum, conference call, or other public speaking engagement including 15 people or more. It also includes meetings with representatives of radio, television, or written print media, including giving interviews and writing articles for print concerning equity recommendations. The term *expressly* does not cover password-protected webcasts or conference calls with existing customers, provided that they have all received the most recent research report containing the necessary disclosures.

RESEARCH ANALYST PROHIBITIONS

Because a research analyst may not participate in the efforts to solicit investment banking business, the following list contains more specific activities that they are prohibited from taking part in:

1. Road shows related to an investment banking service transaction
2. Communications with current or prospective customers in the presence of personnel from the investment banking department
3. Communications with current or prospective customers in the presence of company management if the topic of conversation includes investment banking services

PUBLISHING RESEARCH REPORTS AND MAKING PUBLIC APPEARANCES PROHIBITIONS

Members may not publish or distribute research reports if the member acted as a manager or comanager of an initial public offering (IPO) in the previous 40 days or a secondary offering in the previous 10 days. These same time frames apply to research analysts making public appearances relating to a subject company. Members who have or are participating as an underwriter or dealer of an IPO may not publish a research report or make a public appearance related to that company for 25 days after the date of the offering. Last, any member who is subject to a lock-up agreement may not make a public appearance or distribute a research report related to the issuer in the 15 days leading up to and following the expiration of the lock-up time period.

TERMINATION OF RESEARCH COVERAGE

When a company decides to no longer cover a particular company, it must give notice of the pending termination. The final research report must be made using the same dissemination means it would ordinarily use and provide the customer with all of the same research details that are typically included. The report must also provide a final recommendation or rating unless doing so is impractical (e.g., the research analyst covering that sector has left the firm). If it cannot provide a specific recommendation, the company must disclose the rationale for the decision to terminate coverage of the subject company.

INVESTMENT SUITABILITY

The following is a list of the items that a broker–dealer must know about a customer at a minimum to determine whether a particular investment is suitable:

1. Customer's age
2. Other holdings in the customer's portfolio
3. Overall financial situation (including net worth and overall income needs)
4. Tax status (bracket, filing status, state tax rate, and capital loss carryforward)
5. Investment objectives (growth, aggressive growth, income, and capital preservation)
6. Investment experience (i.e., how advanced have the holdings been in the past)
7. Investment time horizon (i.e., how long until needed to pull from the portfolio as a source of cash flow)
8. Risk tolerance

ROLE OF A PRINCIPAL

Every organization is required to have a principal. This individual's responsibilities include performing due diligence to learn the essential facts about each customer, order, margin position, and each person holding power of attorney over any account held at the organization. This individual supervises all registered representatives of the organization and approves the opening of accounts either before or at the time a customer transaction is completed.

AFFILIATE

The term *affiliate* relates to any person who controls, is controlled by, or is in common control with a member firm. Specifically, it includes the following:

1. An officer, director, or partner who owns 50 percent of the equity interest in a member firm or whose vote represents at least 50 percent of the total
2. Any person who owns 10 percent of the equity interest in a member firm or whose vote represents at least 10 percent of the total
3. Any person including the immediate family members of officers, directors, or partners who own 10 percent of the equity interest in a member firm or whose vote represents at least 10 percent of the total.

DIRECT PARTICIPATION PROGRAM

A *direct participation program* is one in which the tax consequences pass through to the underlying owner's tax return, regardless of the structure of the program (i.e., if an individual purchases an interest in one of these programs, the tax consequences pass through to his or her Form 1040). Examples of this type of program include oil and gas programs, cattle programs, and agricultural programs. Specifically excluded are real estate investment trusts, tax-qualified pension plans, and individual retirement accounts (IRAs).

SUITABILITY REQUIREMENTS

For a sales agent to purchase a direct participation program interest for a customer, suitability must first be established. This includes the following:

1. Determine that the customer is in a financial position to understand the structure of the program, including the tax consequences.
2. Determine the customer is capable of understanding benefits of a direct participation program as laid out in the prospectus.
3. Determine that the customer has enough liquid assets to ensure that immediate liquidity will not be required from the direct participation program.

BROKER–DEALERS RESTRICTIONS

A broker–dealer may not sell a new issue to a customer who is considered a restricted person due to his or her beneficial interest in the company. In addition, the broker–dealer may not purchase a new issue for a customer who has a beneficial interest in the company. These limitations do not apply to the following instances:

1. A company registered under the Investment Company Act
2. A common trust fund that meets the requirements described in the Exchange Act
3. A fund that has investments from at least 1,000 accounts
4. A fund that does not limit the beneficial interests in the fund principally to the trust accounts of restricted individuals
5. The general, separate, or investment account of an insurance company, so long as there are at least 1,000 policy holders
6. An insurance company that does not limit the beneficial interests in the fund principally to the trust accounts of restricted individuals
7. An account where the beneficial interest of restricted individuals does not make up an aggregate of 10 percent of the account value
8. A publicly traded entity that is listed on a national securities exchange or is a foreign issuer
9. An Employee Retirement Security Act benefits plan

10. A state or municipal government benefits plan
11. A tax-exempt charitable organization
12. A church plan

DISTRIBUTION OF A COVERED SECURITY SUBJECT TO A RESTRICTED PERIOD

A member acting as manager of the distribution of a covered security that is subject to a restricted period under Securities & Exchange Commission (SEC) Regulation M is required to provide the following information to the Financial Industry Regulatory Authority (FINRA):

1. Determination of whether the restricted period is one or five days in keeping with SEC Regulation M rules
2. Date upon which the restricted period will lift
3. Names of any distribution participants and affiliated purchasers subject to the restricted period
4. Pricing of the distribution, including the number of shares offered and last sale before the distribution, the basis for the price, and the trade date
5. Cancellation of any distribution in which prior notification of commencement of the restricted period was submitted

DISTRIBUTION OF AN ACTIVELY TRADED SECURITY

A member acting as manager of the distribution of an actively traded security is required to provide the following information to the Financial Industry Regulatory Authority (FINRA):

1. Determination that no restricted period applies and the basis for the determination using Securities & Exchange Commission (SEC) Regulation M as evidence
2. Pricing of the distribution including the number of shares offered, the offering price, the last sale before distribution, the basis for the price, and the trade date
3. Names of the distribution participants and affiliated purchasers

SHORT SELLING A PUBLIC OFFERING

It is unlawful to sell short a security that is currently part of a public offering if the short sale is executed during the shorter of these time frames:

1. Five business days before the pricing of the security, ending the day of the pricing
2. The initial filing of the registration statement, ending with the day of the pricing

BONA FIDE PURCHASE EXCEPTION RULE

The *bona fide purchase exception* states that a person is permitted to purchase shares subject to a public offering to satisfy a short sale transaction if all of the following conditions are met:

1. The number of shares purchase is at least equal to the shares in the short sale transaction.
2. The purchase takes place during regular trading hours.
3. The purchase is reported to an effective transaction reporting plan.
4. The trade took place after the last Rule 105 restricted period short sale and no later than the business day prior to the date of pricing.
5. The short sale is not reported to an effective transaction reporting plan within the 30 minutes prior to the close of regular trading hours on the day prior to the date of pricing.

SEPARATE ACCOUNT EXCEPTION

The *separate account exception* states that the purchase of shares of a public offering in the account of a person where the shares were sold short during the Rule 105 restricted period is permissible if the transaction takes place in a separate account where the trades for each account are made separately without coordination or cooperation between managers.

PUBLIC OFFERING SHORT SALE EXEMPTION

An investment company that is registered under the Investment Company Act of 1940 is permitted to purchase an offered security if the short sale during the Rule 105 restricted period took place in one of these situations:

1. By an affiliated investment company or any series of such a company
2. In a separate series of the investment company

SECURITIES & EXCHANGE COMMISSION (SEC) REGULATION M
AVERAGE DAILY TRADING VOLUME

For Regulation M purposes, the term *average daily trading volume* means the worldwide average daily trading volume for the two full calendar months occurring immediately before the filing of the registration statement or any 60 consecutive calendar days ending within 10 calendar days of the filing of the registration statement. In the event that there is no registration statement, the two full calendar months or 60 consecutive calendar daytime period will be based on the date the offering price is determined.

RESPONSIBILITIES OF THE DISTRIBUTION PARTICIPANT

A distribution participant must do the following:

1. Maintain and enforce written policies and procedures with the goal of ensuring that the flow of information to or from an affiliate that might result in a violation are avoided.
2. Obtain an independent assessment as to the effectiveness of the policies and procedures.
3. Ensure that the affiliate does not share any officers or employees with the distribution participant
4. Ensure that the affiliate does not act as a market maker or engage in solicited transactions in covered securities during the applicable restricted period

PURCHASE LIMITATION FOR A PASSIVE MARKET MAKER IN A COVERED SECURITY

On each day of a Securities & Exchange Commission (SEC) Regulation M Restricted Period, a passive market maker's net purchases may not be greater than either 30 percent of the average daily trading volume or 200 shares in totality. A passive market maker may make one final purchase that, when fully executed, results in exceeding the purchase limitation amount. At the point in which the passive market maker meets or exceeds the purchase limitation amount, he or she must immediately withdraw the quotations.

MAXIMUM STABILIZING BID AND INITIAL STABILIZING BID

The *maximum stabilizing bid* is the lower of the offering price or the stabilizing bid for the security in the principal market (if the principal market is closed, then the stabilizing bid at the previous day's close should be used).

After quotations have been opened for a security in the principal market, an *initial stabilizing bid* may be entered at a price that is not greater than the last independent transaction price (whether that be the same day or the last one on the previous day) if the current ask price is equal to or greater than the last independent transaction price.

INITIATING A STABILIZING BID IN A CLOSED MARKET

When the principal market for a security is closed, but it is before the opening of quotations, the stabilizing bid may be initiated, but the price may not be higher than the lower of the price at which stabilizing could have taken place at the previous close or the most recent price at which the security was traded since the close of the principal market.

When the principal market for the security is closed, but the opening of quotations has already occurred, the stabilizing bid may not be higher than the lower of the price at which the stabilizing bid could have taken place at the previous close or the last independent transaction price if the security traded in the market that day or on the previous business day if the current ask price is equal to or greater than the last independent transaction price.

If there is no market for a security, then the stabilizing bid may not exceed the offering price.

ADJUSTING A STABILIZING BID PRICE

Stabilizing bids may be reduced at any time regardless of any market conditions. A stabilizing bid may also be increased, but only to a price equal to the highest current independent bid, if the market is open, or the highest independent bid at the end of the previous trading day, if the market is closed. In the case that the security is not listed in U.S. dollars, the stabilizing bid may be adjusted in consideration of changes in the exchange rate. If there is a distribution (i.e., right, warrant, or dividend), the stabilizing bid is reduced by the amount of the distribution.

SECURITIES & EXCHANGE COMMISSION (SEC) REGULATION M RULE 104
STABILIZING THE BID ON A SECURITY OUTSIDE THE UNITED STATES

In general, stabilizing bids on securities that are not offered in the United States are in violation of Securities & Exchange Commission (SEC) Regulation M. However, in the event that the United States has a regulatory agreement or statute with the country that issued the security, specifying that stabilizing is a permissible activity, the maximum stabilizing bid will be at a price equal to the current offer price or offer price at the end of the previous business day if the market is not currently open.

STABILIZATION RULES

Securities that meet Rule 144A criteria and are being sold to qualified institutional investors or individuals not from the United States are the only ones that are exempt from the Securities & Exchange Commission (SEC) Regulation M Rule 104 stabilizing rules. A person wishing to receive exempt status on any other type of security may request a ruling by filing a written petition with the Commission. In response, the commission may fully grant, outright deny, or partially the request. Partial approval generally means that it will only pertain to a certain class of securities or transaction type.

INFORMATION REQUIRED TO BE RECORDED WHEN STABILIZING A SYNDICATE OR GROUP OR IMPOSING A PENALTY BID

A person who acts as a manager and stabilizes a syndicate or group or imposes a penalty bid must record the following information:

1. The name and class of the security stabilized or on which a penalty bid was imposed
2. The price, date, and time at which the stabilized bid or penalty bid took place
3. The names and addresses of the members of the group or syndicate
4. The commitments or the percentage participation of each member in the group or syndicate

SYNDICATE OR SELLING GROUPS RULES

Members or those associated with a syndicate or selling group are not allowed to offer covered securities at a reduced price to anyone who is not a member of the syndicate or selling group or of the underwriter. This rule applies to those affiliated with a syndicate group and those affiliated with an underwriter as well.

FINANCIAL INDUSTRY REGULATORY AUTHORITY (FINRA) ARBITRATION

Financial Industry Regulatory Authority (FINRA) arbitration must be used in the following scenarios:

1. Arbitration is required by written (signed) agreement, involves a member of FINRA, and involves securities.
2. The dispute results from a broker's securities activities, and the brokerage firm and the broker are FINRA members. (Note that this is required only for security activity; disputes involving discrimination or other harassment are not required to be arbitrated unless specifically mentioned in an employment agreement or other signed contract.)

21 BOOKS OR RECORDS BROKER–DEALERS ARE REQUIRED TO KEEP FOR A PERIOD OF SIX YEARS

The books or records that each broker–dealer is required to keep for a period of six years are these:

1. *Blotters*—these are daily records detailing all sales and purchases, receipts and disbursements of cash, receipts, and deliveries of securities, including names and dates
2. *Ledgers*—these are records detailing all capital accounts, assets and liabilities, and income and expenses
3. *Ledgers account*—this is a listing of all pertinent information on a per-customer basis, detailing the debits and credits, sales and purchases, and deliveries of securities, including any that are outstanding
4. Ledgers that detail outstanding security transfers including any that have failed to deliver, dividends and interest received, securities, or money loaned or borrowed
5. Ledgers that detail long and short positions for each security, including clearance dates and a log of where each security is physically or electronically held
6. Memos listing the specific instructions given or received related to the purchase or sale of securities, including changes and cancellations of orders
7. Memos listing purchases and sales, including price and time of execution for the account of each member, broker, or dealer
8. Trade confirmations for all purchases and sales
9. Margin records, including the name and address of the owner of any account with an outstanding cash or security margin position
10. Derivative records, including all puts, calls, spreads, and straddles specifically identifying the units involved
11. Trial balance records detailing the aggregate debts and net capital, updated a least once a month
12. A completed employment application for each person associated with a member or broker–dealer, which includes: name (including other names used), address, social security number, date of birth, 10 years of employment history, information about disciplinary actions, and arrests
13. Fingerprints for all securities personnel
14. Agreements between reporting institutions and all inquiry confirmations sent from the Commission

15. A record of each customer with access to the internal system
16. Daily trading summaries, including executed transactions, share volume, and settlement amounts
17. A record related to each account holder, including the name, tax ID number, address, telephone number, date of birth, employment information, annual income, net worth, and investment objectives, including risk tolerance. The customer needs to confirm the information in intervals that do not exceed 36 months.
18. Records listing any written complaints received, including confirmation that the customer was given the contact information for the department to which the complaint should be directed
19. A record listing any purchases or sales that are made to someone associated with a member or broker–dealer where the purchase or sale is intended to be compensation
20. A record demonstrating compliance with advertising rules and regulations
21. Contact information for the individuals in each office who can provide details about the types of records kept and how to access them

Eight Books or Records Broker–Dealers Are Required to Keep for a Period of Three Years

The books or records that a broker–dealer is required to keep for a period of three years are these:

1. All checkbooks, bank statements, cancelled checks, and cash reconciliations
2. Copies of all bills receivable or payable, paid or unpaid, related to the broker–dealer's business
3. Originals of all communications received and copies of all communications sent by the broker–dealer—this includes internal memos relating to the business
4. All trial balances, calculations of aggregate indebtedness and net capital, financial statements, branch office reconciliations, and internal audit papers related to the broker–dealer's business
5. All guarantees of accounts and powers of attorney or other evidence provided to grant any discretionary authority over an account and copies of resolutions allowing an agent to act on the behalf of a corporation
6. All written agreements entered into by the broker–dealer related to the business, including agreements related to any accounts
7. All notices related to an internal broker–dealer system provided to the customers of the broker–dealer who sponsors the system
8. Records containing information used to support the annual financial statements including the following:
    a. Money balance position (both long and short), including both cash and quantity, price, and valuation of each security in any type of account (secured, partly secured, fully secured, or securities accounts payable) for both customers and noncustomers
    b. Amount of secured demand notes and a detailed description of collateral securing demand notes, including the name, quantity, and price for each security or cash securing the note
    c. Descriptions of futures commodity contracts, including market values and gain or loss positions
    d. Description of spot commodity positions in customer and noncustomer accounts
    e. Description of any put and call options, including any that are not in the money
    f. Description of all securities in an account that has an outstanding margin balance

CLOSE-OUT RULE AND THE EXCEPTIONS

In general, a securities contract that has not been completed by the seller may be closed by the buyer no sooner than the third business day following the delivery date. The exceptions to this rule include the following:

1. A contract that is subject to the buy-in requirements of a national securities exchange or a registered clearing agency in which case written notice must be delivered to the seller no later than noon (Eastern Standard Time) two business days in advance
2. Securities transactions that are exempt under Section 3 of the Exchange Act
3. Municipal securities transactions that meet the definition under Section 3 of the Exchange Act
4. Redeemable securities transactions issued by companies registered under the Investment Company Act of 1940

FAILURE TO DELIVER A CONTRACT WITH A BUY-IN NOTICE

In the event that a clearing corporation fails to deliver a contract with a buy-in notice, the contract must still be closed out. This is accomplished by having the broker–dealer purchase the necessary underlying securities at the best price available in the market for the account of the buyer. This may be all of the securities listed in the contract or just a few, if the seller does in fact have some of the underlying securities in one of the accessible accounts.

ACCEPTING PAYMENT FOR SECURITIES PURCHASED OR DELIVERY OF SECURITIES SOLD

The conditions that must be met in order for a broker–dealer to accept an arrangement wherein payment for securities purchased or delivery of securities sold is made to or by the agent of the customer are these:

1. Before or at the time of accepting the order, the customer provided the name and address of the agent.
2. Each order accepted from the customer is notated to acknowledge that it is a payment on delivery or collect on delivery transaction.
3. By the end of the day following the execution of the trade, the broker–dealer delivers a trade confirmation to the customer.
4. The customer provides an agreement indicating that the agent has been giving instructions for the receipt or delivery of the securities and that the agreement includes the following:
5. In a collect-on-delivery transaction, the agent will send the payment by the close of business on the second business day following the trade.
6. In a payment-on-delivery transaction, the agent will deliver the securities by the close of business on the first day following the trade.

TRANSFER PROCEDURES

When a customer wishes to transfer his or her account to another institution, the following needs to occur:

1. The customer completes a transfer instruction form and provides it to the broker–dealer who will receive the assets.
2. That broker–dealer will submit the transfer instruction form to the firm that is currently holding the assets.
3. The carrying firm has one day to validate the instructions by providing the broker–dealer with a statement reflecting all positions and balances carried in the account, at which point the carrying firm has three days to initiate the account transfer.

4. If the carrying firm is unable to validate the instructions, it must provide the broker–dealer with the rationale why the account cannot be transferred in its current form. Once any issues are worked through, the carrying firm has three business days to initiate the account transfer.

DENIAL OF TRANSFER OF AN ACCOUNT TO ANOTHER INSTITUTION

The reasons that the carrying firm may turn down a request to transfer a customer's account to another firm include the following:

1. Additional documentation is needed (death certificate, divorce decree, or marriage certificate).
2. The account does not contain any assets.
3. The account number is incorrect.
4. It is a duplicate request.
5. To transfer the account would violate the carrying firm's credit policy.
6. The customer rescinds the instruction in writing.
7. The social security number on the transfer instruction form does not match the one that the carrying firm has on file.
8. The account title on the transfer instruction form does not match the one that the carrying firm has on file.
9. The transfer instruction form is incomplete or was signed by the incorrect person.
10. The account contains proprietary assets that are not eligible for transfer.
11. The customer has taken possession of the assets in the account.

THREE-DAY ACCOUNT TRANSFER DELIVERY RULE EXCLUSION

The following securities are excluded from the account transfer rule requiring that a carrying firm initiate transfer of account assets within three days of validating the request:

1. Annuity contracts
2. Stripped coupons
3. When-issued or when-distributed securities

CLEARLY ERRONEOUS TRANSACTION

A *clearly erroneous transaction* is one where there is an obvious error in any part of the transaction, including the number of shares (or other unit of trading), the price, or the identification of the security. A transaction that is considered to be clearly erroneous either will be cancelled by both parties involved or will be determined by the Financial Industry Regulatory Authority (FINRA) and subsequently removed from the consolidation tape.

CLEARLY ERRONEOUS TRANSACTION REVIEW

A clearly erroneous transaction can be determined in two different ways. The first is if a senior Financial Industry Regulatory Authority (FINRA) official determines that there has been a malfunction in the electronic communication systems requiring that certain transactions be nullified. In the second scenario, when a member receives confirmation that an order was submitted and believes it falls under the clearly erroneous definition, the member has 30 minutes to submit written notice to FINRA's Market Regulation Department. For routed executions to other market centers, members will be permitted an additional 30 minutes to submit a complaint. In certain circumstances known as *outlier transactions,* FINRA will in its discretion consider complaints submitted after the 30-minute mark but before 60 minutes has passed. To meet FINRA's definition of an outlier transaction, one of the following must be true:

1. The execution price for the security is at least three times the numerical guidelines as referenced under FINRA Rule 11890.
2. The execution price is higher than the 52-week high.
3. The execution price is lower than the 52-week low.

FINRA officials will make a determination as to the validity of the clearly erroneous transaction claim usually within 30 minutes of receipt of the written notice but certainly by opening hour of the next trade day.

CLEARLY ERRONEOUS TRANSACTION EXCHANGE-LISTED SECURITY RULES NUMERICAL GUIDELINES

For a clearly erroneous transaction on an exchange-listed security to be granted by the Financial Industry Regulatory Authority, the price must fall outside the reference price range. The reference price is equal to the consolidated last sale before the execution, with the exception of a multi-stock event involving at least 20 securities.

Reference Price, Circumstance, or Product	Regular Trading Hours Numerical Guidelines	Preopening and After-Hours Trading Session Numerical Guidelines
Greater than $0.00 up to and including $25.00	10 percent	20 percent
Greater than $25.00 up to and including $50.00	5 percent	10 percent
Greater than $50.00	3 percent	6 percent
Multi-stock event (involving at least five securities but less than 20, in less than a five-minute period)	10 percent	10 percent
Multi-stock event -involving more than 20 securities in less than a five-minute period	30 percent	30 percent
Leveraged exchange-traded funds (ETF)/exchange-traded notes (ETN) Securities	Regular trading numerical guidelines multiplied by the leverage multi-plier (e.g., two times)	Regular trading numerical guidelines multiplied by the leverage multiplier (e.g., two times)

A CLEARLY ERRONEOUS TRANSACTION APPEAL REVIEW REQUEST

In the event a member believes that a review of the Financial Industry Regulatory Authority's (FINRA's) clearly erroneous transaction decision is warranted, the member may appeal to the Market Operations Review Committee (MORC). The appeal must be made in writing and received within 30 minutes of the original FINRA decision. Once received, the counterparty will be notified of the appeal request, and both parties will have an opportunity to submit any supporting materials that the committee will need to make its decision. The committee will respond with its determination usually the same trading day, but should the appeal request be received after 3:00 p.m. Eastern Time, the response may not occur until the beginning of the next trading day.

FEES FOR FILING UNSUCCESSFUL CLEARLY ERRONEOUS COMPLAINTS

There are no fees for clearly erroneous complaints resulting in a trade being broken up. However, during each calendar month, a member may only submit two unsuccessful clearly erroneous complaints without being charged any fees. For any complaints beyond the initial two, the member will be charged $250 for every unsuccessful complaint during the remainder of the calendar month. These fees are charged on each security involved in the complaint. For example, if a member has already filed two unsuccessful complaints, and in the same calendar month, the member files a multi-stock complaint involving 20 securities, and the Financial Industry Regulatory Authority (FINRA) does not find in his or her favor, a separate $250 fee will be assessed for each of the 20 securities involved in the complaint. No fee will be assessed if the member withdraws the complaint prior to FINRA's review. For each appeal to the Market Operations Review Committee (MORC), the member will be charged $500 if the committee upholds the original FINRA official's decision. No fee will be assessed should the committee reverse the decision.

CLEARLY ERRONEOUS TRANSACTION OVER-THE-COUNTER SECURITY RULES NUMERICAL GUIDELINES

For a clearly erroneous transaction to be granted by the Financial Industry Regulatory Authority (FINRA), the price must fall outside the reference price range. The reference price is equal to the consolidated last sale immediately before the execution, with the exception of a multi-stock event involving at least 20 securities. The following chart provides specific details:

Reference Price	Numerical Guidelines (Subject Transaction's Percent Difference from Reference Price)
$0.9999 and under	20 percent
$1.00 up to $4.9999	Low end of range minimum 20 percent
	High end of range minimum 10 percent
$5.00 up to $74.9999	10 percent
$75.00 up to $199.9999	Low end of range minimum 10 percent
	High end of range minimum 5 percent
$200.00 up to $499.9999	5 percent
$500.00 up to $999.9999	Low end of range minimum 5 percent
	High end of range minimum 3 percent
$1,000 and over	3 percent

TYPES OF SECURITIES EXCLUDED FROM FEDERAL INCOME TAXATION

The interest on the following types of securities is excluded from federal income taxation:

1. Any security issued or guaranteed by the United States
2. Any security issued by any territory of the United States
3. Any security issued by any state of the United States (including the District of Columbia)
4. Any political subdivision of a state or territory
5. Any security issued by or representing an interest in the Federal Reserve Bank
6. Any interest or participation in any common trust fund or similar fund that does not constitute an investment company
7. Industrial development bonds

CONDITIONS FOR SECURITIES OFFERED THROUGH THE MAIL TO EXEMPT REGISTRATION

The Securities & Exchange Commission (SEC) does not require securities offered through the mail to be registered if they meet the following conditions:

1. The issuer will be doing business only with customers in the state in which the issuer is based.
2. The issuer will not do any business with nonresidents of the state (i.e., those who own vacation homes or are visiting the state and are domiciled elsewhere).

OFFERS AND SALES PART OF THE SAME UNDERLYING ISSUE

The following factors should be considered when determining if offers and sales are part of the same underlying issue:

1. Are the offerings financed under a single plan?
2. Are the offerings for the same class of securities?
3. Are the offerings being made at (or about) the same time?
4. Will the consideration being received be the same?
5. Is the general purpose for the offerings the same?

TYPES OF RESIDENTS EXEMPT FROM REGISTRATION

An issuer may consider the following types of residents when determining whether they qualify for a registration exemption:

1. For a corporation, limited partnership (LP), or limited liability company (LLC), in what state were the articles filed?
2. For a Schedule C business, in what state is the principal office located?
3. For an individual, in what state is the individual's principal residence?

DOING BUSINESS WITHIN A STATE

An issuer will be determined to be doing business within a state if all of the following conditions are met:

1. At least 80 percent of the issuer's gross revenue came from the state in the most recent fiscal year (or if this is the first year of business, during the first six months of the current fiscal year).
2. The issuer had at least 80 percent of its assets located within the state.
3. The issuer intends to use at least 80 percent of the net proceeds in the rendering of services or goods within the state.
4. The principal office is located within the state.

REGISTRATION EXEMPTIONS

Under Regulation A, issuers do not need to register if the offering is less than $5 million in securities in a 12-month period, including no more than $1.5 million offered by security holders of the company. Under the Jumpstart Our Business Start-Ups (JOBS) Act, it was proposed that Regulation A be expanded to include a two-tier system. The old Regulation A exemption would be known as Tier 1. Tier 2 would consist of offerings of up to $50 million in a 12-month period, including no more than $15 million offered by security holders of the company. The following additional requirements would be necessary to qualify for Tier 2 status:

1. Each investor would be restricted to the greater of 10 percent of his or her annual income or 10 percent of his or her net worth.
2. The financial statement included in the offering circular must be audited. 3. The issuer is required to file semiannual reports and current event updates that are similar to the public company reporting requirements. 4. The issuer cannot already be a Securities & Exchange Commission (SEC) reporting company.
3. The issuer cannot have plans to merge or be acquired by an unidentified company. 6. The issuer cannot be selling asset-backed securities in oil, gas, or other mineral rights.
4. The issuer cannot have filed ongoing reports during the previous two years. 8. The issuer cannot be subject to an SEC revocation of registration during the previous five years.

PRIVATE PLACEMENT MEMORANDUM (PPM), CONFIDENTIALITY AGREEMENT, TEASER, AND SUMMARY TERM SHEETS

1. A *private placement memorandum (PPM)* is a legal document used to give the issuer the chance to explain all potential risks to an interested investor. It is used to protect the issuer in the event a disclosed risk actually occurs.
2. A *confidentiality agreement* is between the underwriter and the potential investor; it is a promise not to share underwriting materials. This is because, from a regulatory perspective, many offerings can be made only to those with a verified net worth, risk tolerance, or investment background.
3. A *teaser* is a one-page document that describes the offering to grab the attention of perspective investors. It is often referred to an *executive summary*.
4. A *summary term sheet* is a document that is often designed to include bullet points outlining the pertinent terms and conditions of an offering. A term sheet may be either a proposal or a binding agreement.

TRANSACTIONS TO WHICH SECTION 5 OF THE SECURITIES EXCHANGE ACT (SEA) DOES NOT APPLY

Securities Exchange Act (SEA) Section 5 applies in most circumstances; however, it does not apply to the following:

1. Transactions by anyone who is not an issuer, underwriter, or dealer
2. Transactions by an issuer who is not involved in a public offer
3. Transactions by a dealer, except in the following circumstances:
4. Those taking place within the 40-day period after the first day upon which the security was offered to the public
5. Those where a registration statement was filed within the 40-day period after the first day upon which the security was offered to the public
6. Those where the dealer is acting as a distribution participant and is selling the unsold allotment of subscription

FINANCIAL INDUSTRY REGULATORY AUTHORITY (FINRA) ARBITRATION

Arbitration may be used to settle cases that involve the following:

1. Disputes between an investor and either an individual or entity registered with Financial Industry Regulatory Authority (FINRA) where the claim is filed within six years from the event causing the dispute
2. Disputes between individuals or entities registered with FINRA where the claim is filed within six years from the event causing the dispute

CONFIRMATION OF AN INDIVIDUAL'S ACCREDITED INVESTOR STATUS

An individual's accredited investor status can be confirmed through the following means:

1. For income, Form W-2, 1099, Schedule K-1, or a Filed Form 1040
2. For net worth, bank statements, brokerage statements, or other confirmable documentation from within the last three months
3. A written confirmation from a registered broker–dealer, a Securities & Exchange Commission (SEC)-registered investment advisor, a licensed attorney, or a certified public accountant (CPA) stating that steps have been taken to confirm that the individual or couple meets accredited investor status

PRIVATE PLACEMENT

The following requirements need to be satisfied for a private placement to be in keeping with Regulation D:

1. All investors must have accredited investor status.
2. All investors must have access to the information that would appear in a Securities & Exchange Commission (SEC) registration statement were one to be filed.
3. All parties involved in the private placement must take steps to make sure that all information given to the investors is accurate and as complete as possible so that the investor may adequately perform his or her due diligence.
4. All investors must have access to any pertinent current information about the issuer.
5. All investors must purchase the private placement to be held in their own portfolios. It cannot be sold to another investor.

NOTICE OF SALES

An issuer in a private placement is required to file a notice of sales with the Securities & Exchange Commission (SEC) no later than 15 calendar days after the first sale (unless the 15th day would be a weekend or a holiday, in which case the time frame is extended to the next business day). Should any information in this filing be incorrect, the issuer must file an amendment unless the error relates to an address, aggregate net asset value, or a change in the minimum investment amount of not more than 10 percent.

RULE 505 EXEMPTIONS UNDER THE SECURITIES ACT OF 1933

Securities that meet the following conditions of Rule 505 are exempt from the provisions of Section 5 of the Securities Act of 1933:

1. The aggregate offering price for an offering of securities cannot exceed $5 million less the aggregate offering price for all securities sold within the prior 12 months. So, for example, if an issuer sold $3 million on May 2, 2015, and an additional $500,000 on June 1, 2015, the issuer would only be permitted to sell an additional $1.5 million until May 1, 2016.

2. There cannot be more than 35 purchasers of the securities.

RULE 506 EXEMPTION UNDER THE SECURITIES ACT OF 1933

Securities that meet the following conditions of Rule 506 are exempt from the provisions of Section 5 of the Securities Act of 1933:

1. There are no more than 35 purchasers of the securities.
2. All purchasers are accredited investors.

FINANCIAL INDUSTRY REGULATORY AUTHORITY (FINRA) ARBITRATION PROCESS

The order of the arbitration process is as follows:

1. A claim is filed that details the facts and the requested remedy.
2. The respondent files a statement answering the claim detailing all necessary facts and available defenses to the claim.
3. An arbitrator panel is selected to hear the case.
4. The arbitrator panel meets with the parties involved to schedule hearing dates and go through any preliminary issues.
5. There is a period of discovery in which an exchange of documents and information about the claim takes place.
6. There are hearings in which the parties and arbitrators meet to present arguments and evidence in support of their positions.
7. The arbitrators take time to deliberate the facts and ultimately render a written decision.

RESALE OF A SECURITY QUALIFICATION FOR AN EXEMPTION UNDER RULE 144A

For the resale of a security to qualify for an exemption under Rule 144A, it must meet the following conditions:

1. The security to be sold is only offered to a qualified institutional buyer (or to someone acting on the behalf of one).
2. The seller makes sure that the purchaser realizes that he or she intends to utilize Section 5 of the Exchange Act to justify the sale.
3. The security to be sold is the same class as that which is listed on a national exchange.
4. The security to be sold is not owned by an open-end investment company, a unit investment trust, or a face-amount certificate company.

DESIGNATED OFFSHORE SECURITIES MARKET

The term *designated offshore securities market* means the eurobond market and any foreign securities exchange or nonexchange market designated by the Securities & Exchange Commission (SEC). The features that the Commission takes into consideration when deciding whether to give the designation of offshore securities market are these:

1. Organization under foreign law
2. Association with a recognized community of broker–dealers, banks, or other professional intermediaries
3. Oversight by a governmental or self-regulatory body
4. Oversight standards set by an existing body of law
5. Reporting of securities transactions on a regular basis to a governmental or self-regulatory body
6. System for exchange of price quotations through common communications media
7. An organized clearance and settlement system

DIRECTED SELLING EFFORTS

Directed selling efforts means activity that is undertaken for the purpose of conditioning the market in the United States for securities being offered in accordance with Regulation S. The activity includes placing advertisements in publications that will be generally circulated within the United States. *General circulation* is defined as any publication printed for distribution in the United States and has an average circulation of 15,000 or more copies per issue. An advertisement that is placed under United States or foreign law and specifically references that the securities have not yet been registered under the Securities Act does not constitute direct selling.

A U.S. PERSON

A *U.S. person* is any of the following:

1. Any person residing in the United States
2. Any partnership or corporation that is organized or incorporated in the United States
3. Any estate where the executor is a U.S. person
4. Any trust where the trustee is a U.S. person
5. Any agency or branch of a foreign entity located in the United States
6. Any nondiscretionary account held by a dealer or other fiduciary for the benefit of a U.S. person
7. Any discretionary account held by a dealer or other fiduciary for the benefit of a U.S. person

SALES DEEMED AS HAVING OCCURRED OUTSIDE THE UNITED STATES

A sale will automatically be deemed as having occurred outside the United States if all the following occur:

1. Sales are made in an offshore transaction.
2. No directed selling efforts are made in the United States by the issuer, a distributor, or any person acting on their behalf.
3. The securities are issued by a foreign issuer who believes that there is no substantial U.S. market interest in the particular type of securities being offered.

RULE 144 OF THE SECURITIES ACT OF 1933

RESTRICTED SECURITIES AND CONTROL SECURITIES

A *restricted security* is one that is received in a private sale directly from the issuing corporation or an affiliate of the issuing corporation. Generally, these are acquired as part of an employee equity plan such as restricted stock, stock options, or stock purchase plan. A controlled security is one that is owned by someone affiliated with a corporation, such as a senior executive, director, or a stock holder that owns a very large number of shares.

HOLDING PERIOD PRIOR TO SELLING RESTRICTED SECURITIES IN THE MARKETPLACE

If the issuing company of a restricted security is a reporting company, then it must be held for at least six months prior to disposition. A reporting company is one that that must follow the requirements for reporting under the Securities Exchange Act of 1934. If the issuing company is not a reporting company, the shares must be held for at least one year before they may be disposed. If a restricted security is transferred to another individual as a gift, the recipient may use the original holder's acquisition date to determine when the shares may be sold.

MAXIMUM NUMBER OF SHARES PERMITTED TO BE SOLD

An affiliate is only permitted to sell up to 1 percent of the outstanding shares of the same class in the same three-month period. However, if the stock is listed on a stock exchange, the number of shares that can be sold will be the greater of 1 percent or of the average weekly trading volume for the four weeks leading up to the 144 sale. Over-the-counter (OTC) stocks must use the 1 percent formula.

FORM 144 FILING REQUIREMENT

If in any three-month period an affiliate sells restricted stock cumulatively valued at more than $50,000 or more than 5,000 shares, the affiliate must file a Form 144. An amended Form 144 must be filed in the event that the affiliate does not sell the securities within three months of filing the original Form 144.

INITIAL LISTING STANDARDS FOR A PENNY STOCK

The initial listing standards for a penny stock include the following:

1. Shareholder equity that exceeds $5 million
2. Market value of at least $50 million for the 90 days leading up to the application date, or net income of at least $750,000 during the most recent complete fiscal year, or in two of the last three years
3. The issuer who is in business for at least one year or a market value that exceeds $50 million
4. A stock price of at least $4

GENERAL INITIAL LISTING STANDARDS TO BE LISTED ON THE NEW YORK STOCK EXCHANGE

There are four different standards that an issuer can use to meet the initial listing requirements with the New York Stock Exchange:

1. $750,000 in pretax income, $3 million in public float market value, $4 million in shareholder equity, and a $3 minimum price
2. $15 million in public float market value, 2 years of operating history, $4 million in shareholder equity, and a $3 minimum price
3. $50 million in market capitalization, $15 million in public float market value, $4 million in shareholder equity, and a $2 minimum price
4. $75 million in market capitalization (or $75 million in assets and $75 million in revenue), $20 million public float market value, and a $3 minimum price

GENERAL INITIAL LISTING STANDARDS TO BE LISTED ON THE NASDAQ EXCHANGE

There are four different standards that an issuer can use to meet the initial listing requirements with the NASDAQ exchange:

1. $11 million in pretax earnings aggregated over the past three fiscal years where none of the years was less than $0 and each of the last two years was greater than $2.2 million, and a $4 minimum price
2. $27.5 million in cash flows aggregated over the past three fiscal years where none of the years was less than $0, average market capitalization of $550 million over the past 12 months, $110 million in revenue during the previous fiscal year, and a $4 minimum price
3. $850 in average market capitalization over the past 12 months, $90 million in revenue during the previous fiscal year, and a $4 minimum price
4. $160 million in market capitalization, $80 million in total assets, $55 million in stockholder equity, and a $4 minimum price

Mergers and Acquisitions, Tender Offers, and Financial Restructuring Transactions

PARACHUTE PAYMENT

A *parachute payment,* often called a *golden parachute,* is where a payment is equal to or greater than the aggregate present value (using a discount rate equal to 120 percent of the applicable federal rate compounded semiannually) of the base payment made to an individual and is made in one of the following scenarios:

1. There is a change in the ownership or control of the corporation.
2. There is a change in the ownership of a substantial portion of the assets of the corporation.

HART-SCOTT-RODINO ACT

The Hart-Scott-Rodino Act, also known as the Premerger Notification Program, requires companies to provide the Federal Trade Commission (FTC) and the Department of Justice (DOJ) with information about large acquisitions and mergers before they take place. The companies involved in the merger or acquisition may not finalize their agreement until the waiting period outlined in the law has passed (unless the government allows the deal to close sooner). Generally, the waiting period begins on the day the FTC and DOJ receive notification from all involved parties and ends 30 days later.

FAIRNESS OPINION

A *fairness opinion* is a report that analyzes the details of a merger or acquisition to determine the appropriateness (i.e., fairness) of the acquisition price. These opinions are put together by analysts and advisors who generally work for investment banks. The opinions are created for a fee and are generally requested by key decision makers. A fairness opinion can be requested regardless of whether the companies involved are publicly or privately traded.

DISCLOSURE REQUIREMENTS THAT MUST BE MADE IN FAIRNESS OPINIONS

Certain disclosures are required when issuing fairness opinions:

1. If the firm has acted as a financial advisor to any party analyzed in the fairness opinion
2. If the firm will receive compensation at the completion of the merger or acquisition
3. If any material relationship existed between the firm and either party analyzed in the fairness opinion during the prior two years
4. If substantial information used to create the fairness opinion was supplied by either company that is a subject in the fairness opinion
5. Whether the fairness opinion was approved by a fairness committee
6. Whether the fairness opinion expresses an opinion about the fairness of the compensation to any directors, officers, or employees

FAIRNESS OPINIONS PROCEDURES

The procedures that a company issuing fairness opinions must establish include the following:

1. The circumstances or types of transactions in which the company is willing to issue fairness opinions
2. The process that will be used to select individuals to be part of the fairness committee
3. The qualifications that individuals serving on the fairness committee must meet

4. The process to ensure that a balanced review by the fairness committee takes place
5. The process to ensure that the valuation analyses used by the fairness committee are appropriate

SECURITIES ACT RULE 145

Securities Act Rule 145 details when a sale or offer to sell has occurred. The scenarios under which Securities Act Rule 145 is applicable include the following:

1. Substituting one security for another, not including changes in par value or stock splits
2. Mergers or consolidations in which securities of one company will be exchanged for securities of another
3. Transfer of securities from one individual or company in exchange for the issuance of securities from another

THREE CONDITIONS UNDER WHICH A MEMBER WILL NOT BE DEEMED TO BE ENGAGED IN A DISTRIBUTION

A member must meet one of the three conditions to not be deemed to be engaged in a distribution:

1. The seller of the securities waited at least 90 days from the date of acquisition and did not violate any parts of Rule 144.
2. The member has not been associated as an affiliate of the issuer for at least three months, the issuer is subject to the reporting requirements under the Securities Exchange Act of 1934, and at least six months have passed since the date of acquisition.
3. The member has not been associated as an affiliate of the issuer for at least three months, the issuer is not subject to the reporting requirements under the Securities Exchange Act of 1934, and at least one year has passed since the date of acquisition.

REGULATION M-A
SUMMARY SHEET INFORMATION

The six pieces of information that must be included about a subject company according to Regulation M-A are these:

1. The name, phone number, and address of the subject company
2. The exact title and number of outstanding shares
3. The principal market in which the shares are traded and the high and low sales prices for each quarter during the past two years—if there is no principal market, then the range of high and low bid quotations and the source of them
4. The frequency and amount of any dividends paid during the past two years
5. The date of the offering, the amount of securities offered, and the offering price per share for any prior public offerings during the past three years
6. The range of prices paid and the average purchase price per quarter for any securities purchased during the past two years

SPECIFIC TERMS DISCLOSED IN THE EVENT OF A TENDER OFFER

The terms that must be disclosed in the event of a tender offer are these:

1. The total number and specific class of securities sought in the offer
2. The type and amount of consideration offered to security holders
3. The date upon which the offer will expire
4. Whether a subsequent offering period will be available

5. Whether the offer may be extended (and if so, how)
6. The dates before and after which security holders may withdraw securities tendered in the offer
7. The procedure for tendering and withdrawing securities
8. The manner in which securities will be accepted for payment
9. In the event the offer is for less than all securities outstanding, the periods for accepting securities on a pro-rata basis and the intentions in the event the offer is oversubscribed
10. An explanation of any material differences in the rights of security holders as a result of the transaction
11. A statement explaining the accounting treatment of the transaction
12. The federal income tax consequences for those participating in the transaction

SPECIFIC TERMS DISCLOSED IN THE EVENT OF A MERGER

The seven specific terms that must be disclosed in the event of a merger are these:

1. A brief description of the transaction
2. The consideration offered to security holders
3. The reasons for engaging in the transaction
4. The vote required to approve the transaction
5. An explanation of any material differences in the rights of security holders as a result of the transaction
6. A statement explaining the accounting treatment of the transaction
7. The federal income tax consequences of the transaction

SPECIFIC EVENTS IN WHICH DISCLOSURE OF ANY NEGOTIATIONS, TRANSACTIONS, OR MATERIAL CONTACTS DURING THE PRIOR TWO YEARS MUST BE MADE

The six specific events for which any negotiations, transactions, or material contacts took place during the prior two year period must be disclosed are these:

1. Merger
2. Consolidation
3. Acquisition
4. Tender offer
5. Election of the subject company's directors
6. Sale or other transfer of substantial assets to the subject company

SPECIFIC OUTCOMES FOR WHICH A COMPANY MUST DESCRIBE THEIR PLANS

The specific outcomes for which a company must describe their plans are these:

1. A merger, reorganization, or liquidation involving the subject company or any of its subsidiaries
2. A purchase, sale, or transfer of significant assets of the subject company or any of its subsidiaries
3. A material change in the dividend rate or policy
4. A material change in the indebtedness or capitalization
5. A change in the board of directors or the management of the subject company
6. A change in the company's corporate structure or business
7. The delisting of any class of equity securities
8. The eligibility of any class of equity securities for termination of registration
9. The suspension of the subject company's obligation to file reports

10. The acquisition of additional securities or the disposition of securities
11. Changes in the subject company's charter, bylaws, or governing instruments

SOURCE OF THE FUNDS BEING USED TO COMPLETE TRANSACTIONS

The specific information that a company must include regarding the source of the funds being used to complete its transaction includes the following:

1. The specific source and total amount of funds to be used in the transaction
2. The material conditions to the financing, including any backup plans in case primary financing falls through
3. An itemized statement of all expenses expected to be incurred from the transaction
4. A summary of each loan agreement if any of the funds are borrowed

FINANCIAL STATEMENTS

A company must make available the following financial statements:

1. Audited financial statements for the previous two fiscal years
2. Unaudited balance sheets, comparative year-to-date income statements and related earnings per share data, and statements of cash flow
3. Ratio of earnings to fixed charges for the previous two fiscal years
4. Book value per share according to the most recent balance sheet provided

UNLAWFUL PRACTICES RELATED TO TENDER OFFERS AS LAID OUT IN RULE 14E-1

The following practices are specifically referenced in Rule 14e-1 as being unlawful:

1. Holding a tender offer open for less than 20 business days (60 days if the tender offer involves a roll-up transaction)
2. Increasing or decreasing the percentage of the securities being sought or the payment offered unless the offer remains open for at least 10 business days from the date that notice of the increase or decrease is published or sent to security holders
3. Failure to promptly pay security holders or return the securities deposited
4. Extend the length of the tender offer, unless the extension is made by 9:00 a.m. Eastern Time on the next business day after the scheduled expiration date

DETERMINATION OF SHARES

To determine the number of shares that are available for participation in a tender offer, the individual's net long position must be calculated. *Net long position* is determined by subtracting the individual's short position shares from his or her long position shares.

Long position shares include those that the agent has title to, has purchased but has not yet received, has exercised a standard call option for, and is entitled to receive upon conversion or exchange of an equivalent security.

Short position shares include those that have been sold but not yet delivered, those that are borrowed, and those that are the subject of a written call option that may be exercised by the purchaser of the option.

COVERED PERSON IS NOT PERMITTED TO PURCHASE OR ARRANGE TO PURCHASE ANY SUBJECT SECURITIES RELATED TO A TENDER OFFER

EXCEPTIONS TO THE RULE

The exceptions to the rule that a covered person may not purchase or arrange to purchase any subject securities related to a tender offer are these:

1. Exchanges or exercises of subject securities if the covered person owned the securities prior to the announcement of the tender offer
2. Purchases for plans arranged by an independent agent
3. Odd-lot offers
4. Purchases made as an intermediary (agency basis or as principal so long as the member is not a market maker)
5. Basket transactions, so long as the basket contains at least 20 securities and the covered security does not make up more than 5 percent of the value of the basket
6. Purchases made to satisfy a short sale transaction, so long as the short sale was entered into before the tender offer was announced
7. Purchases in accordance with contractual obligations that are binding and were entered into before the tender offer was announced
8. Purchases by an affiliate of the dealer, so long as there are written policies to keep information from flowing to the affiliate and the affiliate does not share any employees or personnel with the covered dealer
9. Purchases by exempt market makers or exempt principal traders, so long as the issuer is a foreign private issuer and the tender offer is subject to the United Kingdom's City Code on Takeovers and Mergers
10. Purchases during cross-border tender offers
11. Purchases pursuant to a foreign tender offer
12. Purchases by an affiliate of the covered financial advisor, so long as the subject company is a foreign private issuer

BANKRUPTCY CREDITOR PAYMENT ORDER

Corporate creditors are paid in the following order:

1. Secured creditors are paid out first. This includes banks that made loans where tangible property was put up as collateral. If the company had any secured bondholders, they would be paid out at this time as well.
2. General creditors are paid out next. This includes vendors and suppliers of the goods and services provided by the bankrupt company. This category also includes bondholders as this represents a debt of the company.
3. Preferred stock holders are third.
4. Stockholders are last in line. This is because they are owners of the company. The more money the company makes, the more the investment tends to be worth; however, in the event of a corporate failure, they often receive pennies on their initial investment because all creditors are paid out first.

General Securities Industry Regulations

NATIONAL ASSOCIATION OF SECURITIES DEALERS (NASD)

ELIGIBILTY FOR MEMBERSHIP

In general, individuals who are registered as a broker or dealer (including those specializing in municipal or government securities) under the laws of the United States are eligible for membership in the National Association of Securities Dealers (NASD). To become a member, the individual completes an application. The application contains an agreement to follow all federal securities laws, including any decisions made by the NASD. The application also requires that the applicant pay all dues and assessments on a timely basis.

MEMBERSHIP STATUS FOR A REGISTERED MEMBER CALLED INTO ACTIVE DUTY

If a registered National Association of Securities Dealers (NASD) member volunteers or is called into active duty with the United States Armed Forces, his or her membership will be put into inactive status. Upon return to work, there is no need to reregister with the NASD. While serving with the armed forces, the member is eligible to receive transaction-related compensation, including commissions, and is exempt from completing continuing education requirements until he or she returns to active employment status.

ITEMS THAT MUST BE INCLUDED WITH THE FIRM'S APPLICATION

The items that must be included with the firm's Financial Industry Regulatory Authority (FINRA) membership application include the following:

1. Form NMA
2. An original signed and notarized paper form BD
3. An original FINRA-approved fingerprint card for each associated person
4. A new member assessment report
5. A detailed business plan that describes all aspects of the business, including any plans to expand the business in the future, specifically the following:
   a. Trial balance, balance sheet, and computation of net capital prepared within 30 days before the filing date of the application
   b. Monthly projection of income and expenses
   c. Organizational chart
   d. Intended location of the principal place of business and any other offices
   e. List of all securities to be sold or offered
   f. Description of methods to be employed to develop a customer base
   g. Number of markets to be made and anticipated maximum inventory
6. A copy of any decision by federal or state authority taking permanent or temporary adverse action related to the applicant
7. A list of all associated persons
8. Documentation of any regulatory actions against the application, any civil actions for investment-related damages, and customer complaints that require Form U4 reporting
9. Description of any special training or heightened supervision required by a state or federal authority
10. Copy of final or proposed contracts with banks, clearing entities, or service bureaus
11. Description of the applicant's source of capital
12. Description of financial controls to be used by the applicant
13. Description of the applicant's supervisory system and a copy of its written procedures

14. Description of the experience and qualifications of the supervisors and principals as well as anyone who will be supervising personnel
15. Description of the applicant's proposed record-keeping system
16. Copy of the applicant's written training plan to be compliance with continuing education requirements
17. FINRA Entitlement Agreement Program

REJECTION OF MEMBERSHIP REVIEW PROCESS

If Financial Industry Regulatory Authority (FINRA) rejects a membership application, the applicant has 25 days to file a written request with the National Adjudicatory Council for a review of the decision. The request must address why the applicant believes that the decision is not consistent with the membership standards. Within 10 days of filing the request, FINRA will submit the documents that were submitted with the initial application to the National Adjudicatory Council. The council will subsequently form a subcommittee to review the request. This subcommittee will consist of at least two people who are current or past members of the council or former directors or governors. The subcommittee will hold a hearing within 45 days of the filing request. The hearing will be recorded, and a transcript will be prepared by a court reporter. The subcommittee will present a recommendation in writing to the National Adjudicatory Council within 60 days after the hearing date.

APPROVAL OF CHANGES TO A MEMBER'S OWNERSHIP STRUCTURE

In the following situations, a Financial Industry Regulatory Authority (FINRA) member must file an application to approve changes to its ownership structure:

1. A merger with another firm, unless they are both members of the New York Stock Exchange (NYSE)
2. Direct or indirect acquisition by another firm, unless the acquiring firm is a member of the NYSE
3. Direct or indirect acquisition of at least 25 percent of the member's assets, unless the acquiring firm is a member of the NYSE
4. Change in the equity ownership that results in one person or entity having at least 25 percent equity
5. A material change in the business operations

AREAS OF A FIRM'S ENTERPRISE IN WHICH A LIMITED PRINCIPAL MAY BE APPOINTED

A limited principal may be appointed to be responsible for only a portion of a firm's activities. These include the following:

1. Limited principal—financial and operations
2. Limited principal—investment company and variable contracts products
3. Limited principal—direct participation programs
4. Limited principal—registered options and security futures
5. Limited principal—general securities sales supervisor
6. Limited principal—government securities

REPRESENTATIVE

A *representative* is anyone who is associated with the member and works in the investment banking or securities business. This includes those who supervise, solicit, and train personnel associated with any of these functions. Individuals who perform solely administrative support functions (i.e., secretarial duties) are exempt from registration.

REPRESENTATIVE RESPONSIBILITY IN AREAS OF A FIRM'S ACTIVITIES

A limited representative may be appointed to be responsible for only a portion of a firm's activities. These include the following:

1. Limited representative—investment company and variable contracts products
2. Limited representative—direct participation products
3. Limited representative—options and security futures
4. Limited representative—corporate securities
5. Limited representative—equity trader
6. Limited representative—government securities
7. Limited representative—private securities offerings
8. Limited representative—investment banking

MANIPULATION AND DECEPTION ACCORDING TO SECURITIES EXCHANGE ACT (SEA) RULE 10B-5

The three unlawful activities include the following:

1. Utilizing any device or scheme in an attempt to perpetuate fraud
2. Providing any statements that are misleading, materially inaccurate, or lacking of material facts
3. Taking part in a business practice that results in fraud or deceit

DUTY OF TRUST ACCORDING TO SECURITIES EXCHANGE ACT (SEA) RULE 10B5-2

A duty of trust exists in the following circumstances:

1. When one party expressly agrees to keeping information privately or in confidence
2. When the party supplying material, nonpublic information has an expectation of privacy due to a relationship that exists in which the regular sharing of confidential information has occurred
3. When the party receiving material, nonpublic information is the spouse, parent, child, or sibling of the party supplying it, unless it can be established that there was no expectation of privacy.

PURPOSE OF THE SECURITIES EXCHANGE ACT RULE 10B5-1

Securities Exchange Act Rule 10b5-1 deals with the sales and purchases of securities while an individual is in possession of material, nonpublic information, whether the information is about the security itself or the company. The rule lays out the only two permissible defenses to a potential violation of the rule.

PERMISSIBLE DEFENSES TO A POTENTIAL MATERIAL, NONPUBLIC INFORMATION VIOLATION

One of the permissible defenses is where the individual in possession of the material, nonpublic information is able to prove that before receiving or learning the information, he or she entered into an official written plan or binding contract that meets one the following conditions:

1. The plan or contract specifies the exact number of shares to be transacted, the price, and the date on which the transaction is to take place.
2. The plan or contract has an algorithm or formula that, when followed, determines the exact number of shares to be transacted, the price, and the date on which the transaction is to take place.

3. The plan or contract does not allow the individual to have any control over whether the transaction takes place, including the price and the date on which the transaction is to take place

ONE PERMISSIBLE DEFENSE TO A POTENTIAL MATERIAL, NONPUBLIC INFORMATION VIOLATION

One of the permissible defenses is when someone other than the person in possession of the material, nonpublic information is making investment decisions and takes steps to ensure that his or her transaction decisions are in no way influenced by information that might be known by the account owner (e.g., the account is discretionarily managed by an investment advisor who makes the same transactions for all accounts).

OFFICE OF SUPERVISORY JURISDICTION (OSJ) SUPERVISORY ROLES

Within each office of a member firm, the Financial Industry Regulatory Authority (FINRA) requires that at least one person be designated as the office supervisory jurisdiction (OSJ) for that particular location. In some cases, it is necessary for an office to have more than one OSJ. The factors that should be considered to determine the number of OSJs an office should have are as follows:

1. The number of representatives and other associated persons working in the office
2. Whether the registered representatives engage in retail sales involving regular contact with the public
3. Whether a substantial number of registered representatives conduct securities activities at the location
4. Whether the location is close to other firm offices
5. Whether the security activities are diverse or complex

NATIONAL ASSOCIATION OF SECURITIES DEALERS (NASD)

RULE RELATING TO TAPE RECORDING OF CONVERSATIONS

Each member firm that has individuals who participate in telemarketing activities must establish supervisory procedures to ensure that all staff are in compliance with regulatory policies. The procedures should include tape recording all telephone conversations between registered employees and existing and potential customers. The recordings should be kept for at least three years. During the first two years, the tapes need to be easily accessible. The firm should create procedures to review the tapes in keeping with the size, business, and type of customers served.

INTERNAL INSPECTIONS REQUIRED

Each member must conduct an internal inspection of the business at least annually. This includes inspecting every office of supervisory jurisdiction. In addition, at least every three years, every branch office that does not supervise one or more non-branch locations must be inspected. After each inspection, the member is required to write a review of the inspection. In particular, the inspection should ensure that the following are taking place properly:

1. Safeguarding customer funds and securities
2. Maintaining books and records
3. Supervising of customer accounts
4. Transmitting of funds between customers and the third parties
5. Validating customer address changes
6. Validating changes in customer account information

Anti-Money-Laundering Compliance Program

Every member firm is required to create a written anti-money-laundering program to ensure that it is in compliance with the requirements of the Bank Secrecy Act. On an annual basis, a qualified outside party must be brought in to provide independent anti-money-laundering testing. This rule is not required if the member does not execute transactions for customers. In addition, each member firm is required to provide the Financial Industry Regulatory Authority (FINRA) with the names and contact information for all individuals responsible for monitoring the day-to-day operations and those who provide ongoing training of necessary employees.

Private Security Transactions

A *private security transaction* is any security outside the regular scope of a person's employment, including new security offerings. Those associated with a member firm are not permitted to participate in private securities transactions without getting written prior approval from the member firm. If the participation involves selling compensation and is approved, the transaction is recorded on the books and records of the member, and the member supervises the participation in the transaction as if it were executed on behalf of the firm.

Borrowing Money Against the Account of a Customer

Borrowing money from a customer account is permitted only when the member firm has written procedures allowing borrowing and lending of money between registered persons and customers and, even then, only in the following instances:

1. The customer is an immediate family member.
2. The customer is a financial institution that regularly provides financing to others as a normal course of business.
3. The customer and the registered person are both registered with the same member firm.
4. The lending arrangement is based on a personal relationship with the customer, and it would not have been made if the customer and the registered person had not maintained a relationship outside the broker–customer relationship.
5. The lending arrangement is based on a business relationship (not a broker–customer relationship).

Report of Wrongdoing to the Financial Industry Regulatory Authority (FINRA)

A member must report the existence of any of the following situations to the Financial Industry Regulatory Authority (FINRA) within 30 days of uncovering the wrongdoing:

1. There has been violation of any laws, rules, or regulations involving investments or insurance.
2. There has been a written customer complaint involving theft or misappropriation of funds.
3. Someone associated with the firm is a named defendant in a proceeding involving securities rules or regulations (domestic or foreign).
4. Someone associated with the firm is expelled, suspended, or disciplined by any regulatory organization or is denied membership to a regulatory organization.
5. Someone associated with the firm is indicted, convicted, or pleads guilty to any felony or any misdemeanor involving securities.
6. Someone associated with the firm was a director, controlling stockholder, partner, or officer at a company that had its registration denied or revoked.

SANCTIONS DUE TO VIOLATION OF ONE OR MORE RULES

The Financial Industry Regulatory Authority (FINRA) may impose one or more of the following sanctions on a member who violates one or more of its rules:

1. Censure a member.
2. Impose a fine.
3. Suspend membership.
4. Revoke membership.
5. Suspend a person from associating with all members.
6. Impose a temporary or permanent cease and desist order.
7. Impose any other fitting sanction.

Series 79 Practice Test

1. A research analyst is publishing a research report of Upside Industries and would like to confirm the accuracy of portions of its contents with them prior to making it final. Which of the following describes guidelines they must follow in doing so?

    I. The analyst must send a draft of the report to their own legal department at the same time as they are sending the report to Upside for their approval

    II. If new information received from Upside provides for a change in the report's rating, the analyst is required to supply an explanation for such a change in writing to their legal department

    III. It is allowable to include the report's general summary section in making a submission to Upside for information approval

    IV. When sending portions to Upside for approval, any information regarding rating must be excluded in the submission

    a. II and IV
    b. I and II
    c. III and IV
    d. I, II, III, and IV

2. All of the following would be categorized on an income statement as an operating expense EXCEPT...

    a. Labor costs
    b. Cost of goods sold
    c. Insurance costs
    d. Interest charges

3. Which of the following forms must be submitted annually to the SEC by the company, is much more detailed than their annual report, and contains, among other things, company historical and organizational information?

    a. Form 6-K
    b. Form 8-K
    c. Form 10-K
    d. Form 12-K

4. Which of the following ratios is defined as...

Cash equivalents + short-term investments + accounts receivable / current liabilities

    a. Cash ratio
    b. Quick ratio
    c. Debt-to-equity
    d. Current ratio

5. With exceptions, a company is generally required to file their preliminary proxy statement with the SEC at least ___ days before the company shareholders are given access to it.

a. 10
b. 28
c. 12
d. 14

6. All of the following are true of a company's balance sheet EXCEPT...

a. Utilized in an analysis to determine whether the company is in a position of surplus or deficit
b. Consists of two sections: current assets and current liabilities
c. Offers a financial summary of the company's position at a specific point in time
d. Includes stockholder's equity

7. In determining the most accurate new offering price, which of the following types of information must be gathered and analyzed?

I. Competitor company comparisons
II. Overall indications regarding market climate and direction
III. Sector trends
IV. Publicly disseminated quarterly and annual reports for the company

a. II, III, and IV
b. I, II, III, and IV
c. I and IV
d. I and III

8. Common stock + retained earnings - treasury stock is defined as...

a. Unearned revenues
b. Current assets
c. Stockholder's equity
d. Intangible assets

9. Which of the following statements is NOT true regarding a beneficial owner?

a. Company shares are owned by one individual only for the benefit of another individual(s)
b. The interest this owner may have which allows them to profit from transactions involving these shares is called pecuniary
c. An example of a beneficial owner is a pension plan
d. They will be defined as an "insider" if the amount they own exceeds 10 percent of the company's outstanding shares and accordingly will have restrictions imposed upon them regarding the disposition of those shares

10. Which of the following is made up of three sections: operations, investing, and financing?

a. Balance sheet
b. Income statement
c. Cash flow statement
d. Profit and loss statement

11. FINRA (Financial Industry Regulatory Authority) members must seek approval by application for which of the following alterations made to their ownership structure?

    I. Merger with any other firm
    II. Acquisition by any other firm
    III. Any significant change that may affect their business operations
    IV. An individual or entity moving to possess at least 25% of the firm's equity

    a. I, II, and III
    b. I and IV
    c. I and II
    d. III and IV

12. Specific regulations provide a framework for the borrowing of money between a firm's registered person and a customer. Which of the following describes a circumstance in which that type of borrowing could occur?

    a. If the customer is a close and immediate family member
    b. If the customer is registered with a firm different from that of the member firm and registered person
    c. If the customer is a financial institution
    d. If the primary relationship between the two is that of a broker-customer

13. Which of the following describes a scenario(s) when a duty of trust did NOT exist per the Securities Exchange Act (SEA) Rule 10b5-2?

    I. An individual with material, nonpublic information shares that information with someone who they have a regular and recurring business relationship with, but with whom they have not previously shared such confidential information before
    II. An individual with material, nonpublic information has an established relationship with another individual wherein they have previously shared such information with them on a regular basis
    III. An individual with material, nonpublic information shares that information with their brother with whom they have a regular and communicative relationship
    IV. An individual receiving material, nonpublic information explicitly agrees to not share said information

    a. I and III
    b. I only
    c. II only
    d. III and IV

14. Which of the following is NOT true regarding the National Association of Securities Dealers' (NASD) regulatory policies on the recording of conversations?

    a. A process for reviewing recordings should be established based on firm-specific factors such as its size and types of business conducted.
    b. Tape recordings of conversations must be retained for at least three years.
    c. Phone conversations between registered employees and existing customers must be recorded
    d. Phone conversations with potential customers are not required to be recorded

15. In an effort to measure company JHK's overall profitability, calculate their EPS (earnings per share) utilizing the given information below.

Company JHK:	
Net income:	$2,200,434
Preferred dividend:	$250,000
2014	
Preferred stock:	$4,422,000
Common stock (par value $21):	$2,610,000
2015	
Preferred stock:	$4,422,000
Common stock (par value $21):	$2,610,000

   a. $31.39
   b. $15.69
   c. $9.26
   d. $74.73

16. Which of the following is not a role within a firm that a limited principal may be appointed to?

     I. Government securities
     II. Registered options and security futures
     III. Direct participation programs
     IV. Trading floor supervisor

   a. II and IV
   b. I, II, and III
   c. IV only
   d. I and II

17. All of the following are true regarding registered NASD (National Association of Securities Dealers) members who are called into active military duty EXCEPT...

   a. Re-registration will not be necessary upon their return to work
   b. Until returning to active status they will be exempt from any continuing education requirements
   c. They are entitled to receive all compensation related to exercised transactions that occur while they are on inactive status except commissions
   d. NASD membership will be temporarily placed on inactive status

18. Which of the following is/are TRUE regarding who may be considered an investment banking representative?

     I. Executive level administrative assistant
     II. Sales staff training personnel
     III. Secretary of the firm
     IV. Trading floor supervisor

   a. II and IV
   b. I, II, III, and IV
   c. IV only
   d. I and II

19. Member firms are required by the regulatory policies of the National Association of Securities Dealers (NASD) to perform internal inspections of their business at least every year. Which of the following are point(s) of inspection they must address?

> I. Ensure that there is proper supervision overall customer accounts
> II. Confirmation of the procedures for customer funds to be safeguarded
> III. Confirmation that the process utilized to transmit funds between customers and other third parties is appropriate and secure
> IV. Review of the procedures for the maintenance of the firm's books and records

   a. III only
   b. I, II, III, and IV
   c. II and III
   d. I, III, and IV

20. An analyst would like to measure inventory turnover. Which of the following formulas can be utilized to do that?

> I. $\dfrac{sales}{average\ accounts\ payable}$
> II. $\dfrac{sales}{inventory}$
> III. $\dfrac{cost\ of\ goods\ sold}{average\ inventory}$
> IV. $\dfrac{net\ credit\ sales}{average\ inventory}$

   a. II and III
   b. III only
   c. III and IV
   d. II only

21. The number of Office Supervisory Jurisdiction (OSJ) designations within a given office is determined by all of the following except:

   a. The degree of complexity regarding the investment activities conducted in that office
   b. The office's proximity to other offices of the firm
   c. The number of registered representatives that are participating in investment activities at that office
   d. The number of years registered representatives have been at the given office

22. Which of the following are TRUE of the process for an applicant requesting a review of their rejected application for FINRA (Financial Industry Regulatory Authority) membership?

> I. FINRA, within 10 days, will forward the associated review documentation to the National Adjudicatory Council
> II. Review hearing will be recorded
> III. Applicant must submit a written request for review within 60 days
> IV. Rejected application review will be conducted by the National Adjudicatory Council

   a. I and II
   b. II and III
   c. I, III and IV
   d. IV only

23. The Financial Industry Regulatory Authority (FINRA) requires that members are required to report, within 30 days, certain situations of potential wrongdoing as they become aware of them. Which of the following would they NOT be obligated to report per FINRA regulations?

a. An associate of the firm is denied membership to the National Association of Securities Dealers (NASD).
b. An associate of the firm pleads guilty to a securities related felony.
c. Any written customer complaint regarding a registered person.
d. An associate of the firm is a defendant in a foreign court proceeding regarding a securities regulation violation.

24. Given the following information on company REX, calculate EDITDA (earnings before interest, taxes, depreciation, and amortization).

Revenue from sales:	$889,221
Interest on deposits:	$9,202
Cost of goods sold:	$167,003
Gross profit:	$738,442
Depreciation:	$41,556
Amortization:	$20,776
Income tax payable:	$16,990
Year's annual net income:	$255,007

a. $70,120
b. $343,531
c. $308,137
d. $325,127

25. All of the following are requirements for inclusion on a firm membership application to FINRA (Financial Industry Regulatory Authority) EXCEPT:

a. A firm organizational chart
b. A list of all securities the firm intends to sell
c. A photocopy of a fingerprint card for each associated individual
d. All of the above

26. A limited representative may be assigned responsibilities in all of the following areas of the firm EXCEPT...

a. Options
b. Equity trading
c. Supervising the sale of securities
d. Corporate securities

27. Which of the following are TRUE of a Dividend Reinvestment Plan (DRIP)?

    I. Tax incentives are offered for participation in this plan
    II. It provides for the opportunity to purchase treasury stock shares
    III. Involves utilizing the proceeds of dividend payouts
    IV. Shares are priced at a discount

  a. II, III, and IV
  b. II and III
  c. I, II, III, and IV
  d. I and IV

28. When preparing for participation in a transaction, a company is required to disclose all of the following information regarding the source of funds for that transaction EXCEPT:

  a. Details regarding a backup plan for the source of funding in the event that their planned and primary source of funding fails
  b. If funds are being loaned, summary details of the loan agreements are required regarding those funds
  c. Timing, including specific dates for the disbursal of funds
  d. An itemized statement of all expenses expected to be incurred from the transaction

29. All of the following are true of prefiling period rules EXCEPT...

  a. Content of disclosures is limited to what is traditionally utilized by this issuer
  b. During this period no offers to sell can be made
  c. Disclosures can include valuations, but not projections
  d. Statements of opinion are not allowed

30. All of the following are required to be disclosed in a fairness opinion EXCEPT...

  a. Whether the fairness opinion had received approval from a fairness committee
  b. If the firm had a substantial relationship within the past five years with either parties that are the subject of the fairness opinion
  c. If the firm will be compensated post-acquisition
  d. If the firm has acted as an advisor to parties subjected to analysis within the opinion

31. Characteristics of a "shell company" include all of the following EXCEPT...

  a. Involve no business operations
  b. Are utilized by start-up firms
  c. Maintain minimal assets
  d. Sometimes signal that illegal operations are going on

32. The definition of short position shares includes all of the following EXCEPT...

  a. Shares that have been loaned
  b. Shares that have been purchased but not received
  c. Shares that sellers of a written call option are obligated to be sold to the purchaser of that option providing they choose to exercise their option to purchase them
  d. Shares that have been sold just not delivered yet

33. All of the following are sections found in a registration statement EXCEPT...

a. Financial information and data for the last six fiscal years
b. Code of ethics for the company
c. Notification of any change in accountants during previous two fiscal years
d. Disclosures and analysis regarding market risk

34. In the event of a company merger, which of the following disclosures are required per Regulation M-A?

I. Total number of outstanding shares for companies involved in the transaction
II. Amount and frequency of dividends paid out over the previous year
III. An explanation of the reasons and motivations for participating in the transaction
IV. Necessary vote count for the transaction to be approved

a. I, II, and IV
b. III and IV
c. II and III
d. I and IV

35. Covered persons are prohibited from participating, via either making purchases or arrangements to purchase, securities related to a tender offer. Of the following scenarios, which does NOT qualify as an exception to this rule?

a. Purchase made as a result of a binding contract that was initiated prior to the tender offer
b. Purchase made as a result of a foreign tender offer
c. Offer that is odd-lot
d. An exchange of securities that involves the covered person having obtained said securities after the tender offer announcement

36. A "seasoned issuer"...

a. Issued a minimum of $1 billion in preferred stock over previous three years
b. Issued a minimum of $1 billion in nonconvertible debt over previous three years
c. For the previous 12 months has dutifully and promptly filed its reports
d. For the previous six months has dutifully and promptly filed its reports

37. Which of the following provides for the sale of specific types of securities without having to register them with the SEC prior to the sale, and only after having acquired them via merger, acquisition, or reclassification?

a. Securities Act Rule 145
b. Securities Exchange Act Rule 176
c. Blue Sky Laws
d. Rule 14e-1

86

38. All of the following are scenarios detailing unlawful activities per Rule 14e-1 EXCEPT:

a. Tender offer expiration on Tuesday, May 6, extending the window of the tender offer with notification of the extension occurring at 11:00 a.m. Eastern Standard Time on Wednesday, May 7

b. Window of opening for tender offer held for less than 30 business days

c. Failing to provide payment in a timely manner for securities received, or if nonpayment occurs, failing to return the securities that were received

d. Increasing or decreasing the percentage of the securities being sought or the payment offered unless the offer remains open for at least 10 business days from the date that notice of the increase or decrease is published or sent to security holders

39. Investment company DG would like to disseminate a "generic advertisement." In determining which type of information they may include in it, all of the following types EXCEPT which would be allowable?

a. Invitation for anyone to submit inquiries for further information

b. Description of the type of analysis they could provide along with an example using real world historical data on a current project of theirs

c. Services offered

d. General investment objectives

40. When a team representing an issuer travels around the country making sales presentations to potential analysts and investors, it is referred to as a...

a. Deal flow

b. Package deal

c. Scale out

d. Road show

41. A company is required by Regulation M-A to provide specifics regarding their plans to do all of the following EXCEPT...

a. A change in geographic location for the company headquarters

b. A sale of a considerable amount of their assets

c. A corporate reorganization of one of its subsidiaries

d. A change in management

42. Which of the following are TRUE of a prospectus:

I. May be accompanied by a free writing prospectus

II. Also known as a "red herring"

III. Will reference and detail the operations of a business

IV. Will only be presented in its final form

a. II, III, and IV

b. I, II, and III

c. I, II, III, and IV

d. II and III

43. The Hart-Scott-Rodino Act:

a. Provides for the sale of certain securities without first registering them with the Securities Exchange Commission (SEC)

b. Requires a company to provide advance notice to the Department of Justice (DOJ) and the Federal Trade Commission (FTC) prior to finalizing a large acquisition, merger, or tender offer

c. Provides regulation to prevent manipulative and deceptive practices in relation to stock and securities transactions

d. Sets forth criteria for the determination of, after signing a registration statement, whether an individual had grounds for reasonable belief in the most primary points in that statement

44. Company BTS is a small company that is required to provide a registration statement. Which of the following are items that they must submit?

    I. A list of directors
    II. A description of their company property
    III. Details regarding executive compensation
    IV. Methodology behind the determination of the offering price

a. I, III, and IV

b. III only

c. I, II, and IV

d. I and IV

45. A net long position is calculated by:

a. Taking an investor's long position shares and subtracting their short position shares

b. Taking an investor's short position shares and adding them to their long position shares

c. Taking an investor's short position shares and subtracting their long position shares

d. Doubling an investor's short position shares

46. Per Securities Exchange Act (SEA) Regulation S-X, all of the following are required for filing financial statements EXCEPT...

a. A consolidated financial statement must be filed for subsidiary companies

b. A review of the financial statements must be made by someone who is outside of and unaffiliated with the company

c. A consolidated balance sheet must be filed for the company

d. An attestation report must be filed by the company accountants

47. Regulation M-A requires that a company disclose specific summary sheet information. Which of the following are items they are required to submit?

    I. If subject to previous public offerings over last five years, the per share price for those offerings
    II. Name, address and phone number
    III. Number of outstanding shares
    IV. Quarterly high and low sale prices for the previous year

a. I, II, III, and IV

b. II, III, and IV

c. II and III

d. I and II

48. Company PGL would normally be required to submit five copies of their prospectus to potential investors looking at their offering but have been notified that 10 copies each is what is now required. All of the following are scenarios that would explain the need for the additional copies EXCEPT...

    a. Offering is associated to a security with a delayed basis issuance

    b. Supplemental corrective information is now provided in current prospectus due to errors in the previous prospectus

    c. Market risk for this offering is high given the company and industry involved, and the overall current market climate

    d. Supplemental information is now provided in current prospectus in response to omissions in the previous prospectus

49. A company intending to issue a fairness opinion must look to creating and enforcing all of the following procedures EXCEPT...

    a. Ensuring the fairness committee provides a valuation that is appropriate and fair

    b. Ensuring the fairness committee provides a fair, objective, and balanced review

    c. Determining the qualifications for members of the fairness committee

    d. All of the following procedures are necessary

50. Company BKT's corporate creditors are listed below. In the event they declare bankruptcy, in what order would their creditors be paid, first to last?

    I. Preferred stockholders
    II. Secured creditors
    III. General creditors
    IV. Stockholders

    a. III, II, IV, and I

    b. II, III, I, and IV

    c. II, I, III, and IV

    d. I, II, III, and IV

51. Which of the following would Company PLY utilize in the event of an acquisition?

    a. Form S-8

    b. Form S-1

    c. Form S-4

    d. Form S-3

52. Given issuer rules related to prospectuses, which of the following pieces of information would not be considered allowable for an issuer to communicate to potential investors outside of the prospectus?

    a. Plan for offering proceeds

    b. Security price

    c. Date securities are slated to be offered and available to the public

    d. Non-publicly available information

53. Per Regulation M-A which of the following types of financial statements is a company required to provide?

a. Book value per share as derived from a balance sheet dated the previous year
b. Audited version of company balance sheets
c. Previous three fiscal years' worth of audited financial statements
d. Ratio of earnings to fixed charges for the previous two fiscal years

54. Which of the following statements is TRUE of "golden parachutes"?

I. Utilized by a firm as an anti-takeover measure
II. Can include stock options, but not severance pay
III. Receipt of these benefits would occur only for terminations that are the result of a takeover or merger
IV. Also known as change-in-control benefits

a. I and IV
b. I and II
c. III only
d. I, II, III, and IV

55. The definition of long position shares include which of the following?

I. Shares that have been purchased but for which possession has not yet occurred
II. Shares for which a call option has been exercised for
III. Shares that have been sold but for which possession is still held
IV. Shares for which title is possessed

a. II, III, and IV
b. I and IV
c. I, II, and IV
d. II and IV

56. A company involved in a tender offer has specific disclosures required of them by Regulation M-A which include all of the following EXCEPT...

a. An explanation of the reasons and motivations for participating in the transaction
b. Federal income tax considerations and consequences for all parties of the transaction
c. Whether there is the possibility of the offer being extended
d. Expiration date of the offer

57. A "fairness opinion"...

I. Can only be requested by publicly traded companies
II. Is authored by an investment bank analyst
III. Is utilized to analyze the acquisition price for a merger or acquisition
IV. Is provided free of charge based on a pre-existing business relationship

a. I, II, and IV
b. I only
c. II and III
d. I, II, III, and IV

58. Form S-1 includes all of the following except:

   a. Company's competitors
   b. Plans for offering proceeds
   c. Company business model
   d. Financial disclosures

59. A company entering into which of the following transactions or events will be required to disclose significant contacts, transactions, and negotiations that occurred over the previous two years?

   a. Company's sale of a few small assets
   b. After an acquisition
   c. Removal of one of the company's directors
   d. Merger

60. Companies must look to specific criteria in order to determine whether information they would like to disseminate meets the definition of the term "factual business information." Which of the following are included in that list of criteria?

     I. Issuing company is registered under the Investment Company Act of 1940
     II. Issuing company is a business development company
     III. Information is the type of information traditionally communicated to both current customers and potential investors
     IV. Information to be disseminated has been previously communicated

   a. IV only
   b. I, III, and IV
   c. II and III
   d. I and II

61. An investor is seeking to invest in short-term securities. Which of the following would be appropriate potential investments?

     I. Certificates of deposits (CDs)
     II. Treasury bills
     III. Money market securities
     IV. Repurchase agreements

   a. I and II
   b. I, II, and III
   c. III and IV
   d. I, II, III, and IV

62. A investor seeking to calculate company RZT's return on investment (ROI) would utilize which of the following formulas?

   a. $\dfrac{net\ income}{shareholders'\ equity}$

   b. $\dfrac{net\ income}{total\ assets}$

   c. $\dfrac{net\ income - dividends}{total\ capital}$

   d. $\dfrac{gain\ from\ investment - cost\ of\ investment}{cost\ of\ investment}$

63. The Securities & Exchange Commission (SEC) requires issuers to submit which of the following registration documents?

    a. Three copies of each registration statement amendment
    b. Two copies of any documents filed through the EDGAR system
    c. Four copies of the registration statement itself
    d. Two copies of any proposed underwriting agreements

64. Given the following information on Company PL, calculate their "Forward P/E."

Current trading price per share:	$126
Earnings per share (previous four quarters):	$6
Earnings per share (upcoming four quarters):	$9

    a. $21
    b. $14
    c. $16.80
    d. $8.40

65. All of the following are examples of derivatives EXCEPT...

    a. Call option contract
    b. Callable bond
    c. Put
    d. Forward contract

66. All of the following statements are true regarding transfer instructions EXCEPT...

    a. Instructions must be validated by the carrying company with a statement of the account, and provided within one day
    b. Transfer instruction form is eventually forwarded to the firm holding the assets in the account that are to be transferred
    c. If the carrying firm cannot validate the instructions upon first receipt, the transfer must be cancelled
    d. A transfer instruction form must is filled out by the customer and submitted to the broker-dealer who is to be receiving the transferred account

67. Which of the following factors applies to macroeconomics?

    I. Supply and demand combined with the resulting impact on prices
    II. Gross domestic product
    III. Retail sales
    IV. Employment indicators

    a. II, III, and IV
    b. I and III
    c. I, II, III, and IV
    d. III only

68. An investor owns 300 shares of stock in Company DSY. The stock pays $2.55 in annual dividends and has a current market price of $72.50 per share. Calculate the dividend yield for this investor.

a. 3.5%
b. 4.8%
c. 10.5%
d. 24.2%

69. A "greenshoe option" is…

a. When an issuer and underwriter contract to restrict specific individuals from selling their shares for a specific period of time
b. When an issuer provides an underwriter the right to sell a larger amount of shares than originally negotiated
c. When an offering must be sold out or cancelled
d. When an underwriter contracts to sell the highest amount of an offering that they can

70. Which of the following is defined as the marketplace where new securities are issued and sold directly by an issuer?

a. Over-the-counter (OTC) market
b. Interbank market
c. Primary market
d. Secondary market

71. Utilizing the information below, calculate company PLT's return on assets (ROA) for the year ending June 30, 2015.

Total assets as of July 1, 2014:	$1,133,786
Total assets as of June 30, 2015:	$1,101,224
Annual net income as of June 30, 2015:	$311,004

a. 7.19 percent
b. 27.4 percent
c. 27.8 percent
d. 28.2 percent

72. All of the following would qualify as information that would be considered content for a "forward-looking statement" EXCEPT:

a. Plans for 12-month growth of business operations
b. Earnings per share projections
c. Communicating through an analysis of current operations, the three-year outlook for those continued operations
d. Budgets for future discretionary celebrations

73. The following statements are all true regarding the meaning of the term "emergency" EXCEPT…

a. Significant signs or market indications of extreme price fluctuations occurring in the future do not qualify
b. An interruption in transaction settlements do qualify
c. Sudden market price fluctuations do qualify
d. Significant indications of the processing of transactions being interrupted qualify

74. **Which of the following indicates a company's ability to pay the interest on their total debt?**

    a. Net margin
    b. Interest coverage
    c. Return on investment
    d. Debt-to-equity

75. **Calculate the "dividend payout ratio" for Company SRF using the following information.**

Reported earnings per share over previous year:	$15
Dividend per share payment paid in each of last four quarters:	$1

    a. 26.7 percent
    b. 6.7 percent
    c. 3.8 percent
    d. 15 percent

76. **FINRA requires all of the following pieces of information to be provided electronically except:**

    a. Estimate for the maximum amount to be owed to the underwriter for advisory fees
    b. Descriptions of any relationships that may exist between investors owning five percent or more of the issuer's securities and a director
    c. Estimated maximum offering price
    d. Estimate of the minimum finder's fees

77. **Which of the following is false regarding the measure "enterprise value to sales" (EVS)?**

    a. In general, an investor would like to see a higher EVS in that it would indicate that the company is viewed as overvalued
    b. Provides investors with an idea of how much it would cost to buy the company's sales
    c. A measure that compares a company's enterprise value to their sales
    d. EVS=(market cap + debt + preferred shares – cash and cash equivalents)/annual sales

78. **Broker-dealers are required to keep records of which of the following for three years?**

    a. Copies of any communications sent by them, and original versions of all communications they received
    b. Ledgers containing specifics of income and expenses, assets and liabilities
    c. Blotters detailing daily purchases and sales
    d. Purchase and sale trade confirmations

79. **Calculate inventory turnover for Company LOK given the following information.**

Reported cost of goods sold for the current year:	$2,225,555
Beginning inventory:	$6,550,000
Ending inventory:	$8,990,211

    a. 68
    b. 34.9
    c. 28.6
    d. 49.5

80. A company is being sued as the result of their registration statement allegedly having omitted material and key information. Which of the following individuals may be held to be potentially liable with regards to the lawsuit?

I. Any individual who signed the registration statement

II. Clerical personnel responsible for the physical preparation of the statement, although having not provided any substantive or editorial contribution

III. Appraisers who provided expert contributions to the registration statement's preparation

IV. All current members of the company's board of directors regardless of whether they were on the board at the time of the filing of the statement or not

a. I, III, and IV
b. III and IV
c. I and III
d. I, II, and III

81. Calculate TR Investment Fund's total expense ratio (TER) utilizing the information below.

Total assets:	$1,477,902
Operational expenses:	$133,324
Management fees:	$78,122
Trading fees:	$46,098

a. 9.02 percent
b. 17.43 percent
c. 14.31 percent
d. 5.29 percent

82. In an effort to provide investor protection, the Securities & Exchange Commission (SEC) may require issuers to provide...

a. Records of exercised options for the previous 12-month period
b. Certified profit and loss statements for the previous three fiscal years
c. A list of investors who hold more than 15 percent of the outstanding shares
d. Payments made to directors if in an amount that is in excess of $20,000 per year

83. The formula for enterprise value is:

a. market capitalization + debt + minority interest + preferred shares - total cash and cash equivalents

b. $\frac{\text{current share price}}{\text{sales per share}}$

c. $\frac{\text{closing price of the stock}}{\text{latest quarter's book value per share}}$

d. $\frac{\text{preferred shares+cash and cash equivalents}}{\text{annual sales}}$

84. Which of the following qualify as "underwriting compensation"?

    I. Warrants
    II. Employer benefits (i.e., stock bonuses)
    III. Stock options
    IV. FINRA filing fees

  a. I, II, and III
  b. I, II, III, and IV
  c. I and III
  d. II and IV

85. Which of the following is TRUE of a recession?

  a. Increase in industrial production
  b. Extended downturn
  c. A decline in gross domestic product (GDP) that is less than 10 percent
  d. Unemployment increasing over six successive quarters

86. Calculate the "current yield" on a bond trading at a premium of 115 cents on the dollar and with a coupon rate of 2.5 percent.

  a. 2.47 percent
  b. 2.17 percent
  c. 4.9 percent
  d. 4.6 percent

87. In looking at employee stock options and stock appreciation rights (SARs), which of the following describes the main difference?

  a. Vesting date denotes the time their opportunity to purchase begins
  b. SARs provide the right to purchase specific number of shares at a specific price
  c. When SARs are exercised, employee receives difference between current market price and the strike price
  d. Only employee stock options are part of an employee's compensation package

88. In legally organizing a business, which of the following would provide an entity in which taxation occurs at the corporate level?

  a. C corporation
  b. S corporation
  c. Limited liability company
  d. Limited partnership

89. An investor who is looking to invest in a debt instrument that is not tied to any specific assets and issued by the government could choose which of the following?

  a. Debenture
  b. Rights
  c. Convertible bond
  d. Warrants

90. Which of the following are examples of a "lagging economic indicator"?

    I. Wages
    II. Consumer price index
    III. Gross domestic product (GDP)
    IV. Housing market

    a. I and II
    b. I, III, and IV
    c. III and IV
    d. I, II, III, and IV

91. Asset-backed securities are backed by all of the following EXCEPT…

    a. Company's receivables
    b. Leases
    c. Loans
    d. Mortgages

92. A government security with a five-year maturity would be a:

    a. Treasury note
    b. Treasury bond
    c. Treasury bill
    d. Treasury option

93. The Fed increases the federal funds rate. All of the following statements regarding the potential impact that will have on the economy, Company WT, and its stock are true except:

    a. Businesses are impacted with less demand for their goods and accordingly produce less revenue
    b. Company WT pays higher interest on its debt which negatively affects their bottom line
    c. Individuals with variable rate debt will have less money to spend
    d. More individuals will borrow money

94. Calculate the "bond equivalent yield" for a bond with a $1,000 par value, discounted purchase of $975, and 120 days to maturity.

    a. 7.60 percent
    b. 3.04 percent
    c. 7.79 percent
    d. 9.75 percent

95. An investor would like to put together a portfolio of stocks with market capitalizations between $2 billion and $10 billion. Which of the following categories of stocks should this investor focus on?

    a. Large-cap
    b. Mid-cap stock
    c. Small-cap
    d. Micro-cap stock

96. Which of the following are TRUE of a value stock?

    I. High price-to-earnings ratio
    II. Low dividend yield
    III. Investors view these as having upside and potential to increase in price
    IV. Current market price is lower than what the stock's fundamental information represent it should be

    a. I, III, and IV
    b. II and III
    c. III and IV
    d. I, II, and IV

97. "Rights" are NOT...

    a. Providing the holder with the opportunity to purchase shares only according to the amount of rights they own
    b. Available for an extended period of time before expiring
    c. An entitlement to buy shares at a specific preset price
    d. Priced at a discount to the market

98. Which of the following types of risk is described as the risk that an investor will not be able to buy another bond (once the initial bond matures) that will have interest rates that are equal or greater?

    a. Interest rate risk
    b. Reinvestment risk
    c. Business risk
    d. Credit risk

99. All of the following are true of inflation EXCEPT...

    a. Inflation indicates the degree to which prices in an economy increase over time
    b. An increase in the inflation rate usually means the economy is slowing down
    c. Rise in inflation rate results in individuals having less money to spend
    d. A decrease in the inflation rate signals that prices are decreasing

100. A qualified institutional buyer can be...

    I. An investment company
    II. An employee benefit plan
    III. An entity in which all of the owners are qualified institutional buyers
    IV. An insurance company

    a. I and IV
    b. I, II, III, and IV
    c. III and IV
    d. I and II

Answer Key and Explanations

1. A: A research analyst who is publishing a research report of Upside Industries and who would like to confirm the accuracy of portions of its contents with the company prior to making the report final should follow certain guidelines in doing so. First, if Upside were to provide NEW information in response to the approval request that necessitated a rating change within the report, the analyst would be required to supply an explanation for such a change in writing to their legal department. Second, in sending portions to Upside for approval, any information regarding rating must be excluded in the submission. Third, the analyst must send a draft of the report to their own legal department BEFORE sending the report to Upside for their approval, not simultaneously. Last, it is NOT allowable to include the report's general summary section in making a submission to Upside for information.

2. D: A company's income statement reports both their operating and non-operating activities. Operating activities are those associated with normal business operations. Examples are labor costs, cost of goods sold, and insurance costs. Non-operating expenses are those that are NOT associated with normal business operations. One example is an interest charge.

3. C: Form 10-K must be submitted annually to the SEC by the company, is much more detailed than their annual report, and contains (among other things) company historical and organizational information. Form 6-K is utilized for foreign private issuers of securities and allows for transparency by requiring them to report widely any information reported to their own local securities regulators. Form 8-K is utilized by a company to report specifically unscheduled changes within the company that would be of material importance to either the company's shareholders or the SEC.

4. B: The quick ratio is a liquidity ratio, also referred to as the "acid test ratio," that provides for a more conservative analysis and is defined as: cash equivalents + short-term investments + accounts receivable / current liabilities. The cash ratio is an even more conservative liquidity ratio and is defined as: cash + equivalents + invested funds / current liabilities. The current ratio is the least conservative of the liquidity ratios and is defined as: current assets / current liabilities. The debt-to-equity ratio provides information regarding a company's leverage position and is defined as: company liabilities / shareholders' equity.

5. A: A company is generally required to file their preliminary proxy statement with the SEC at least 10 days before the company shareholders are given access to it. Exceptions to this requirement include but are not limited to having the proxy detailing ONLY information regarding an issued shares increase or the approval of an executive compensation package.

6. B: A company's balance sheet can be utilized in an analysis to determine whether the company is in a position of surplus or deficit and offers a financial summary of the company's position at a specific point in time. It however consists of three sections: assets (current, depreciable, and intangible), liabilities (current and long-term), and stockholder's equity.

7. B: In pricing a new offering, all of the above types of information should and must be gathered and analyzed. The company's competitors should be researched and utilized in a comparative analysis. The company's quarterly and annual reports should be reviewed, and analysis of the company's sector, as well as the climate and direction for the overall market, should be strongly considered.

8. C: Common stock + retained earnings - minus treasury stock is defined as stockholder's equity. Unearned revenues are considered to be a current liability. Current assets are cash, accounts receivable, prepaid items, and inventory, and intangible assets include items such as good will and trade names.

9. D: A beneficial owner who owns an amount of shares that exceeds 10 percent of the company's outstanding shares is NOT considered an insider for the purposes of having restrictions imposed upon them regarding the disposition of these shares. A beneficial owner owns company shares only for the benefit of another individual(s). They may have a pecuniary interest in these shares which would allow them to potentially profit from transactions involving the shares, and an example of a beneficial owner would be a pension plan.

10. C: The cash flow statement is divided into three sections: operations, investing, and financing. It is designed to aid in the analysis of a company's operational performance and efficiency, and utilizes information from both the company's income statement and balance sheet.

11. D: FINRA (Financial Industry Regulatory Authority) members must seek approval by application for any significant change that may affect their business operations, and in the event that an individual or entity moves to possess at least 25 percent of the firm's equity. A merger requires approval only if both firms are not members of the New York Stock Exchange (NYSE), and a firm's acquisition by another firm requires approval only if the acquiring firm is not a member of the NYSE.

12. A: The borrowing of money between a firm's registered person and a customer has specific requirements that must be met in order for such a transaction to occur. Of the circumstances provided, this sort of borrowing could occur given the customer was a close and immediate family member of the registered person. Beyond this, regulations require that both the registered person and customer must be registered with the same member firm, and further, the customer can be a financial institution, but ONLY one that has lending as part of their normal business activities. Also, the PRIMARY relationship between the customer and registered person must be that of an outside business one, not simply a broker-customer relationship.

13. B: Per the Securities Exchange Act (SEA) Rule 10b5-2, a duty of trust does NOT exist where material, nonpublic information is shared with an individual with whom the sharer of the confidential information may have a recurring business relationship, but with whom there is NOT an established practice of sharing this sort of private information previously. A duty of trust DOES exist when an individual with material, nonpublic information has an established relationship with another individual wherein they have previously shared such information with them on a regular basis; when an individual with material, nonpublic information shares that information with their brother with whom they have a regular and communicative relationship; and when an individual receiving material, nonpublic information explicitly agrees to not share said information.

14. D: The National Association of Securities Dealers' (NASD) regulatory policies on the recording of conversations require that conversations between registered employees and BOTH existing and potential customers MUST be recorded. Additionally, a process for reviewing recordings should be established based on firm-specific factors such as its size and types of business conducted, and tape recordings of these conversations must be retained for at least three years.

15. B: EPS (earnings per share) ratio = net income - preferred stock dividends / average shares outstanding

$$EPS = \frac{\$2,200,434 - \$250,000}{\left(\dfrac{\dfrac{\$2,610,000}{\$21} + \dfrac{\$2,610,000}{\$21}}{2}\right)}$$

$$= \frac{\$1,950,434}{\dfrac{124,286 + 124,286}{2}}$$

$$= \frac{\$1,950,434}{\dfrac{248,572}{2}}$$

$$= \frac{\$1,950,434}{124,286}$$

$$= \$15.69$$

16. B: Within a firm, a limited principal may be appointed to head up government securities, registered options and security futures, and direct participation programs.

17. C: Registered NASD (National Association of Securities Dealers) members who are called into active military duty are entitled to receive all compensation related to exercised transactions that occur while they're on inactive status, INCLUDING commissions. Additionally, their membership will be temporarily placed on inactive status, while inactive they will be exempt from any continuing education requirements, and upon returning to work, re-registration will not be necessary.

18. A: A "representative" for these purposes must be employed in the investment banking business performing job duties that are non-administrative in nature. Sales staff training personnel and the trading floor supervisor would qualify here as acting in roles that would be deemed those of an investment banking representative. Both the executive level administrative assistant and secretary would be viewed as having roles that are solely administrative and therefore would NOT meet the definition of representative. Accordingly, they would be exempt from any registration requirements.

19. B: Member firms are required by the regulatory policies of the National Association of Securities Dealers (NASD) to perform internal inspections of their business at least once every year. Point(s) of inspection they must address include ensuring that there is proper supervision overall customer accounts, confirming the procedures for customer funds being safeguarded, confirming that the process utilized to transmit funds between customers and other third parties is appropriate and secure, and reviewing the procedures for the maintenance of the firm's books and records.

20. A: Inventory turnover provides a measure of a company's inventory and how many times it is sold and replaced over time. Of the above choices, two can be utilized by this analyst to measure inventory turnover: 1) sales / inventory, and 2) cost of goods sold / average inventory.

21. D: The number of Office Supervisory Jurisdiction (OSJ) designations within a given office will be determined by the degree of complexity regarding the investment activities conducted in that office, the office's proximity to other offices of the firm, and the amount of registered representatives that are participating in investment activities at that office.

22. A: Regarding the review process for a rejected application for FINRA (Financial Industry Regulatory Authority) membership, FINRA will forward the associated review documentation to the National Adjudicatory Council within 10 days, and the resulting review hearing will be recorded. An applicant however requesting a review of their rejected application for FINRA membership must do so within 25 days, NOT 10, and the rejected application review will be conducted by a subcommittee appointed by the National Adjudicatory Council (NAC), NOT the actual NAC. This subcommittee is required to have at least two current or former council members.

23. C: Given Financial Industry Regulatory Authority (FINRA) regulations, a member would NOT be obligated to report just ANY written customer complaint regarding a registered person. There are SPECIFIC instances that require a member to report, within 30 days, situations of potential wrongdoing as they become aware of them. These include an associate of the firm being denied membership to the National Association of Securities Dealers (NASD), an associate of the firm pleading guilty to a securities related felony, and an associate of the firm being a defendant in a foreign court proceeding regarding a securities regulation violation.

24. D: $BITDA = $ net income $+$ income tax $+$ depreciation $+$ amortization $-$ interest income

$$EBITDA = (\$255,007 + \$16,990 + \$41,556 + \$20,776) - \$9,202$$

$$= \$334,329 - \$9,202$$

$$= \$325,127$$

25. D: There are specific requirements for Financial Industry Regulatory Authority (FINRA) firm membership applications. These include a firm organizational chart, a list of all securities the firm intends to sell, an original copy of a fingerprint card for each associated individual, and the description of the financial controls to be used by the applicant.

26. C: A limited representative may be assigned responsibilities related to only specific activities within a firm. Areas that are allowable are options, equity trading, and corporate securities. They may NOT be assigned responsibilities related to supervising the sale of securities.

27. A: A Dividend Reinvestment Plan (DRIP) provides for the opportunity to purchase treasury stock shares utilizing the proceeds of dividend payouts. The shares are priced at a small discount. Tax incentives however are NOT offered for participation in this plan.

28. C: When preparing for participation in a transaction, a company is NOT required to disclose the timing, including specific dates for the disbursal of funds for that transaction. However, they ARE required to provide details regarding a "plan B" source of funding in the event that their planned and primary source of funding fails, an itemized statement of all expenses expected to be incurred from the transaction, and if funds are being loaned, a summary detail of the loan agreements is required regarding those funds.

29. C: The pre-filing period is the time that starts with finalizing the underwriting agreement and ends with the Securities & Exchange Commission (SEC) registration filing. Disclosures CANNOT include valuations or projections. The content of disclosures is limited to what is traditionally utilized by this issuer, during this period no offers to sell can be made, and any statements of opinion are not allowed.

30. B: It must be disclosed if the firm has had a substantial relationship within the past two years—NOT five—with either parties that are the subject of the fairness opinion. Further disclosures required for inclusion are those stating whether the fairness opinion had received approval from a fairness committee, if the firm will be compensated post-acquisition, and if the firm has acted as an advisor to parties subjected to analysis within the opinion.

31. C: Shell companies involve no business operations, are utilized by start-up firms, and sometimes signal that illegal operations are going on. However, they do NOT maintain any assets within the company.

32. B: The definition of short position shares does NOT include shares that have been purchased but not received. These would be considered long position shares. Short position shares include those that have been loaned, those that the seller of a written call option are obligated to be sold to the purchaser of that option providing they choose to exercise their option to purchase them, and those that have been sold but not delivered yet.

33. A: A registration statement will have several sections, some of which include a code of ethics for the company, notification of any change in accountants that occurred during previous two fiscal years, and disclosures and analysis regarding market risk. It will also include financial information and data for the last five years, NOT six.

34. B: In the event of a company merger, the disclosures required per Regulation M-A include an explanation of the reasons and motivations for participating in the transaction, and the necessary vote count for the transaction to be approved. Disclosures NOT required are the total number of outstanding shares for companies involved in the transaction, and the amount and frequency of dividends paid out over the previous year.

35. D: Covered persons are prohibited from participating, via either making purchases or arrangements to purchase, securities related to a tender offer. Exceptions to this rule include a purchase made as a result of a binding contract that was initiated prior to the tender offer, a purchase made as a result of a foreign tender offer, and an offer that is odd-lot. An exchange of securities that involves the covered person having obtained said securities after the tender offer announcement is NOT an exception to this rule. The exception would only exist if the covered person had obtained the securities PRIOR to the tender offer announcement.

36. C: A "seasoned issuer" is one that has dutifully and promptly filed its reports for the previous 12 months and does not meet the requirements to qualify as a well-known seasoned issuer.

37. A: The Securities Act Rule 145 provides for the sale of specific types of securities without having to register them with the SEC prior to the sale, and only after having acquired them via merger, acquisition, or reclassification. The Securities Exchange Act Rule 176 sets forth criteria for the determination of, after signing a registration statement, whether an individual had grounds for reasonable belief in the most primary points in that statement. Blue sky laws seek to provide protection against securities fraud by requiring sellers to register their offerings and disclose their financial data.

38. B: Per Rule 14e-1, it is NOT unlawful for a tender offer to be held open for less than 30 business days. However, it IS unlawful to hold it open for less than 20 business days. Further, it is unlawful for a tender offer with an expiration of Tuesday, May 6 to be extended if notification of the extension does not occur until 11 a.m. Eastern Standard Time on Wednesday, May 7. It is also unlawful to fail to provide payment in a timely manner for securities received, or if nonpayment occurs, fail to return the securities that were received.

39. B: Investment company DG could disseminate a "generic advertisement" that included the services they offer, their general investment objectives, and an invitation for anyone to submit inquiries for further information. They could NOT include a description of the analysis they provide if, along with it, they utilized an example using real world historical data on a current project of theirs. It is NOT allowable to make reference in any SPECIFIC way to any particular security or investment.

40. D: When a team representing an issuer travels around the country making sales presentations to potential analysts and investors, it is referred to as a road show. Deal flow is a qualitative measure used in investment banking to indicate the degree to which "business" is good or bad, and is largely driven by the state of the economy. A package deal is a market order that involves multiple orders that must either be simultaneously executed or, if not, then not at all. This package of orders is utilized as a tool in executing a specific investment strategy. A scale out involves incrementally selling held shares in portions as the stock price increases. The motivation is to receive and utilize profits as the price increases rather than waiting for the peak to sell an entire position all at once.

41. A: A company is NOT required by Regulation M-A to provide specifics regarding their plans to make a change in geographic location for the company headquarters. However, they ARE required to provide specifics regarding their plans to make a sale of a considerable amount of their assets, initiate a corporate reorganization of one of its subsidiaries, and make a change in management.

42. B: A prospectus, also known as a "red herring," will reference and detail the operations of a business, and may be accompanied by a free writing prospectus. It may be presented, however, in either a preliminary OR final version.

43. B: The Hart-Scott-Rodino Act requires a company to provide advance notice to the Department of Justice (DOJ) and the Federal Trade Commission (FTC) prior to finalizing a large acquisition, merger, or tender offer. The Securities Act Rule 145 provides for the sale of certain securities without first registering them with the Securities Exchange Commission (SEC), and the Securities Exchange Act (SEA) Rule 10b-5 provides regulation to prevent manipulative and deceptive practices in relation to stock and securities transactions. The Securities Exchange Act Rule 176 sets forth criteria for the determination of, after signing a registration statement, whether an individual had grounds for reasonable belief in the most primary points in that statement.

44. B: As a smaller company, BTS is NOT required to submit the detailed information that a larger company would have to. Examples of items they would NOT be required to submit include their list of directors, a description of their company property, and the methodology behind the determination of the offering price. They WOULD be required to submit details regarding the compensation of the executives in their company.

45. A: A net long position is calculated by taking an investor's long position shares and subtracting their short position shares.

46. A: Per Securities Exchange Act (SEA) Regulation S-X, requirements for filing financial statements include a review of the financial statements being made by someone who is outside and unaffiliated to the company, a consolidated balance sheet being filed for the company, and an attestation report being filed by the company accountants. Regulation S-X does NOT require a consolidated financial statement being filed for subsidiary companies, and instead requires SEPARATE financial statements to be filed for subsidiaries.

47. C: Per Regulation M-A, a company must disclose specific summary sheet information such as their name, address, phone number, and the number of outstanding shares. If the company has been subject to previous public offerings over the last three years—NOT five—they must submit the per share price for those offerings, and the quarterly high and low sale prices for the last two years, NOT just the previous year.

48. C: Company PGL would be required to submit 10 copies of their prospectus to potential investors instead of five for any of the following three reasons: first, if their offering was associated to a security with a delayed basis issuance; second, supplemental corrective information was to now be provided in the current prospectus due to errors in the previous prospectus; or third, supplemental information was to now be provided in the current prospectus in response to omissions in the previous prospectus. They would NOT be required to submit the additional copies simply because the market risk for this offering was too high given the company and industry involved, and the overall current market climate.

49. D: A company intending to issue a fairness opinion must look to creating and enforcing procedures that include ensuring the fairness committee provides a valuation that is appropriate and fair; ensuring the fairness committee provides a fair, objective and balanced review; and determining the qualifications for members of the fairness committee.

50. B: Should company BKT declare bankruptcy, the order of payout to their creditors would be their secured creditors first, their general creditors second, the company's preferred stockholders third, and their stockholders last.

51. C: Form S-4 is utilized in the event of an acquisition or merger. Form S-8 is utilized in relation to employee benefit plans and the company stock within them. Form S-1 is utilized in the planning of a public offering. Form S-3 registers securities for a company that has already met other reporting requirements.

52. D: It is allowable for an issuer to communicate certain pieces of information to potential investors outside of the prospectus. These include the company's plan for offering proceeds, the security price, and the date securities are slated to be offered and available to the public. Publicly available factual information such as contact information for the business can be communicated, but information that is not publicly available is not allowed.

53. D: Per Regulation M-A, the types of financial statements a company is required to provide include the book value per share as derived from most recent balance sheet, an unaudited version of company balance sheets, ratio of earnings to fixed charges for the previous two fiscal years, and the previous two fiscal years' worth of audited financial statements.

54. A: "Golden parachutes" refer to the substantial benefits offered to executives at the time of their termination. Utilized by firms as an anti-takeover measure, they are also known as change-in-control benefits. The benefits afforded executives can include stock options, cash bonuses, AND severance pay. A golden parachute benefit package can refer to the lucrative benefits an executive receives as the result of ANY termination of employment but is most commonly attributed to terminations resulting from a takeover or merger.

55. C: The definition of long position shares includes shares that have been purchased but for which possession has not yet occurred, shares for which a call option has been exercised for, and shares for which title is possessed. It does NOT include shares that have been sold but for which possession is still held. These would be considered short position shares.

56. A: A company involved in a tender offer has specific disclosures required of them by Regulation M-A which include the federal income tax considerations and consequences for all parties of the transaction, whether there is the possibility of the offer being extended, and the expiration date of the offer. An explanation of the reasons and motivations for participating in the transaction is NOT a required disclosure for a tender offer.

57. C: A "fairness opinion" is authored by an investment bank analyst or advisor, and is utilized to analyze (checking for "fairness") the acquisition price for a merger or acquisition. The report can be requested by BOTH publicly and privately traded companies, and is authored for a fee, NOT free of charge.

58. D: A Form S-1 is utilized in the planning process for a public offering and includes information regarding a company's competitors, their plans for the offering proceeds, and the company's overall business model.

59. D: Per Regulation M-A, companies are required to disclose significant contacts, transactions, and negotiations occurring over their prior two years of business when participating in the sale of a considerable amount of assets, during an acquisition or merger, and when in the process of electing their slate of company directors.

60. A: Companies must look to specific criteria in order to determine whether information they would like to disseminate meets the definition of the term "factual business information." One item on this list of criteria would be that the information to be disseminated had been previously communicated. Other criteria would include that the issuing company would NOT be registered under the Investment Company Act of 1940; that the issuing company would NOT be a business development company; and that the information be the type of information that is traditionally communicated to current customers, NOT potential investors.

61. D: An investor seeking to invest in short-term securities could choose any of a variety of money market securities. Certificates of deposits (CDs), treasury bills, and repurchase agreements are ALL examples of money market securities.

62. D: $$\text{Return on Investment} = \frac{\text{gain from investment} - \text{cost of investment}}{\text{cost of investment}}$$

$$Return\ on\ Equity\ (ROE) = \frac{net\ income}{shareholders'\ equity}$$

$$\text{Return on Assets (ROA)} = \frac{\text{net income}}{\text{total assets}}$$

$$\text{Return on Investment Capital (ROIC)} = \frac{\text{net income} - \text{dividends}}{\text{total capital}}$$

63. A: With regards to registration documents, the Securities & Exchange Commission (SEC) requires issuers to submit three copies of each registration statement amendment, one copy of which has the indications of the changes that had been made to the statement. They also require one, NOT two copies of any documents filed through the EDGAR system; and three, NOT four copies of the registration statement itself. They require three, not two, copies of any proposed underwriting agreements.

64. B:

$$\text{Forward } \frac{P}{E} = \frac{\text{market price per share}}{\text{expected earnings per share}}$$

$$\text{Forward } \frac{P}{E} = \frac{\$126}{\$9}$$

$$= \$14$$

65. B: Derivatives are contracts between two or more parties and are "derived" from the value of an underlying asset. Examples of these are a call option contract, a put, and a forward contract. A call is a contract that, once entered into, provides for the purchaser the "option" to purchase a security for a specific price, for a specific time, and obligates the seller to sell that security to them for that price until expiration of the contract occurs. A put is a contract that, once entered into, provides for the purchaser the "option" to sell a security for a specific price, for a specific time, and obligates the seller to purchase that security from them for that price until expiration of the contract occurs. A forward contract is a contract entered into between two parties that involves buying or selling an asset for an agreed upon price and at a specified future time. A callable bond is one that allows for the issuer of it to repurchase it at some time over its life and it is NOT considered to be a derivative security.

66. C: A transfer instruction form must is filled out by the customer and submitted to the broker-dealer who is to be receiving the transferred account. A transfer instruction form is eventually forwarded to the firm holding the assets in the account that are to be transferred. Instructions must be validated by the carrying company with a statement of the account, and provided within one day. If the carrying firm cannot validate the instructions upon first receipt, the transfer will NOT be cancelled. An explanation would be provided by the carrying company demonstrating the reason for the inability to validate the account as it is. Upon them validating the account, the carrying company will then begin the transfer within three business days.

67. A: Macroeconomics studies the economy as a whole rather than individual segments or markets. Factors affecting that study are gross domestic product, retail sales, and employment indicators. Supply and demand combined with the resulting impact on prices is a factor that is considered in the study of microeconomics which studies the effects that individual decisions have on the economy.

68. A:

$$\text{Dividend Yield} = \frac{\text{annual per share dividend}}{\text{price per share}}$$

$$\text{Dividend Yield} = \frac{\$2.55}{\$72.50}$$

$$= .0352 = 3.5\%$$

69. B: A "greenshoe option" is when an issuer provides an underwriter the right to sell a larger amount of shares than originally negotiated. A lock-up agreement is when an issuer and underwriter contract to restrict specific individuals from selling their shares for a specific period of time. All or none is when an offering must be sold out or cancelled. Best efforts are when an underwriter contracts to sell the highest amount of an offering that they can.

70. C: A primary market is a marketplace where new securities are issued and sold directly by an issuer. The over-the-counter (OTC) market is where trading occurs for those stocks NOT listed on the NASDAQ, the New York Stock Exchange (NYSE), or the American Stock Exchange (AMEX). The interbank market is where currencies are traded by financial institutions. The secondary market is where investors buy and sell securities amongst themselves.

71. C:

$$\text{Return on Assets (ROA)} = \frac{\text{annual net income}}{\text{average total assets}}$$

$$\text{Return on Assets (ROA)} = \frac{\$311,004}{\frac{\$1,133,786 + \$1,101,224}{2}}$$

$$= \frac{\$311,004}{\frac{\$2,235,010}{2}}$$

$$= \frac{\$311,004}{\$1,117,505}$$

$$= .2783 = 27.8\%$$

72. D: The definition of content for "forward-looking statements" could include plans for 12-month growth of business operations; earnings per share projections; and communicating through an analysis of current operations, the three-year outlook for those continued operations.

73. A: The term "emergency" can apply to actual extreme price fluctuations, AS WELL AS significant signs or market indications of extreme price fluctuations occurring in the future. Additionally, it can be applied to an interruption in transaction settlements, sudden market price fluctuations, and significant indications of the processing of transactions being interrupted in the near future.

74. B: A company's interest coverage ratio will indicate their ability to pay the interest on their total debt. A net margin ratio indicates the degree to which a company's earnings then translate to actual profits. Return on investment takes into account the cost of an investment and then measures the benefit to that investor given that cost. Debt-to-equity demonstrates the proportion of debt and equity that a company utilizes to finance its assets.

75. A:

$$\text{Dividend Payout Ratio} = \frac{\text{yearly dividend per share}}{\text{earnings per share}}$$

$$\text{Dividend Payout Ratio} = \frac{\$1 \times 4}{\$15}$$

$$= \frac{\$4}{\$15} = .2666 = 26.7\%$$

76. D: FINRA requires certain pieces of information to be provided electronically, including an estimate for the maximum amount to be owed to the underwriter for advisory fees, the estimated

108

maximum offering price, and descriptions of any relationships that may exist between a director and any investors owning five percent or more of the issuer's securities.

77. A: The measure "enterprise value to sales" (EVS) provides investors with an idea of how much it would cost to buy the company's sales. It is a measure that compares a company's enterprise value to their sales, and in general, an investor would like to see a lower EVS in that it would indicate that the company is viewed as undervalued. Here is the formula:

$$\frac{\text{market cap} + \text{debt} + \text{minority interest} + \text{preferred shares} - \text{cash and cash equivalents}}{\text{annual sales}}$$

78. A: For three years broker-dealers are required to keep copies of any communications sent by them, and original versions of all communications received by them. Ledgers containing specifics of income and expenses, and assets and liabilities, blotters detailing daily purchases and sales, and purchase and sale trade confirmations are all required to be kept for six years, NOT three.

79. C:

$$\text{Inventory Turnover} = \frac{\text{cost of goods sold}}{\text{average inventory}}$$

$$\text{Inventory Turnover} = \frac{\$2,225,555}{\frac{\$6,550,000 + \$8,990,211}{2}}$$

$$= \frac{\$2,225,555}{\frac{\$15,540,211}{2}}$$

$$= \frac{\$2,225,555}{\$7,770,106}$$

$$= .2864 = 28.6$$

80. C: A company that is being sued as the result of their registration statement allegedly having omitted material and key information will have a variety of individuals who may be held potentially liable with regards to the lawsuit. These include any individuals who signed the registration statement and appraisers who provided expert contributions to the registration statement's preparation. Clerical personnel responsible ONLY for the physical preparation of the statement will not be held liable, having NOT provided any substantive or editorial contribution. Additionally, ONLY members of the company's board of directors who were on the board at the time of the registration statement's fling will be held potentially liable.

81. B:

$$\text{Total Expense Ratio (TER)} = \frac{\text{total funds cost}}{\text{total fund assets}}$$

$$\text{Total Expense Ratio (TER)} = \frac{(\$133,324 + \$78,122 + \$46,098)}{\$1,477,902}$$

$$= \frac{\$257,544}{\$1,477,902}$$

$$= .1743 = 17.43\%$$

82. B: In an effort to provide investor protection, the Securities & Exchange Commission (SEC) may require issuers to provide certified profit and loss statements for the previous three fiscal years. They will NOT require records of exercised options for the previous 12-month period to be provided, but WILL require records for those currently open and those soon to be bought or sold. They will also require the issuer to provide a list of investors who hold more than 10 percent, NOT 15, of the outstanding shares, and notification of any payments made to individuals EXCLUDING directors and officers, if in an amount that is in excess of $20,000 per year.

83. A: Enterprise Value = market capitalization + debt + minority interest + preferred shares − total cash and cash equivalents

$$\text{Price to Sales} = \frac{\text{current share price}}{\text{sales per share}}$$

$$\text{Price to Book Value} = \frac{\text{closing price of the stock}}{\text{latest quarter's book value per share}}$$

84. C: "Underwriting compensation" can include warrants or stock options. Items that do NOT qualify are employer benefits, i.e., stock bonuses and FINRA filing fees.

85. C: A recession is characterized by a decline in gross domestic product (GDP) that is less than 10 percent. Further, it is defined as a temporary, NOT extended economic downturn; and is most noticed by a DECREASE in industrial production, and unemployment increasing over two years, NOT six successive quarters.

86. B:

$$\text{Current Yield} = \frac{\text{annual interest income}}{\text{current bond price}}$$

$$\text{Current Yield} = \frac{2.5}{115}$$

$$= .0217 = 2.17\%$$

87. C: The main difference between employee stock options and stock appreciation rights (SAR's) is that, when exercised, the employee RECEIVES the difference between the current market price and the strike price. The employee does NOT pay the actual strike price as is done with employee stock options. Both are considered part of an employee's compensation package.

88. A: A C corporation is generally taxed at the corporate level. An S corporation has taxation occurring on the personal tax returns of the shareholders, and a limited liability company is defined as having taxation forwarded to the tax returns of the partners.

89. A: A debenture is a debt instrument that is not tied to any specific assets and can be issued by the government. Rights are securities that provide shareholders with the opportunity to purchase a company's newly issued shares. A convertible bond allows for conversion of the bond into a specific number of shares of stock. A warrant provides a debt holder the opportunity to buy a specific number of a company's newly issued shares.

90. A: A lagging economic indicator is one that reflects a change in the economy that has already begun to occur. Examples of these are wages and the consumer price index. Gross domestic product (GDP) is a coincident indicator reflecting the current state of the economy. The housing market is a leading indicator and acts as a predictor of potential future change.

91. D: Asset-backed securities are debt securities and can be backed by leases, loans, and a company's receivables. They CANNOT be backed by mortgages.

92. A: A government security with a five-year maturity would be a treasury note which has maturities that can range from more than one year to less than 10. A treasury bond can have a maturity of more than 10 years and a treasury bill has a maturity of less than one year.

93. D: With the Fed increasing the federal funds rate, individuals with variable rate debt will have less money to spend, they will be discouraged from borrowing money, and businesses will be impacted with less demand for their goods, which will result in a reduced level of revenue for them. Company WT will also pay higher interest on its debt, which will hurt their bottom line.

94. C:

$$\text{Bond Equivalent Yield (BEY)} = \frac{\text{par value} - \text{purchase price}}{\text{purchase price}} \times \frac{365}{\text{days to maturity}}$$

$$\text{BEY} = \frac{\$1,000 - \$975}{\$975} \times \frac{365}{120}$$

$$= \frac{\$25}{\$975} \times 3.0417$$

$$= .0256 \times 3.0417$$

$$= .0779 = 7.79\%$$

95. B: An investor wanting to put together a portfolio of stocks with market capitalizations between $2 billion and $10 billion should turn their focus to mid-cap stocks. Large-cap stocks have market capitalizations of more than $10 billion, small-cap stocks are between $300 million and $2 billion, and micro-cap stocks are between $50 million and $300 million.

96. C: Value stocks have a current market price that is lower than what the stock's fundamental information representing it should be. Investors view these stocks as having upside and a potential to increase in price. Additionally, they characteristically have a high, NOT low dividend yield; and low, NOT high price-to-earnings ratios.

97. B: "Rights" are NOT available for an extended period of time before expiring and instead are available for only a BRIEF time. However, they ARE an entitlement to buy shares at a specific preset price, usually priced at a discount to the market, and provide the holder with the opportunity to purchase shares only according to the amount of rights they own.

98. B: Reinvestment risk is the risk that an investor will not be able (once the bond matures) to buy another bond that will have interest rates that are equal or greater. Interest rate risk involves the decline in value of a debt security that results from interest rates rising. Business risk is the threat that not all companies within a specific industry will experience the same return on investment. Credit risk is the risk that a bondholder will be unable to satisfy their payments on principal and interest.

99. D: Inflation indicates the degree to which prices in an economy increase over time. A rise in inflation rate results in individuals having less money to spend and usually means the economy is slowing down. A decrease in the inflation rate does NOT signal that prices are decreasing, but rather that it is reflecting a SLOWER rate of increase in prices.

100. B: A qualified institutional buyer can be an investment company, an employee benefit plan, an entity in which all of the owners are qualified institutional buyers, and an insurance company.

How to Overcome Test Anxiety

Just the thought of taking a test is enough to make most people a little nervous. A test is an important event that can have a long-term impact on your future, so it's important to take it seriously and it's natural to feel anxious about performing well. But just because anxiety is normal, that doesn't mean that it's helpful in test taking, or that you should simply accept it as part of your life. Anxiety can have a variety of effects. These effects can be mild, like making you feel slightly nervous, or severe, like blocking your ability to focus or remember even a simple detail.

If you experience test anxiety—whether severe or mild—it's important to know how to beat it. To discover this, first you need to understand what causes test anxiety.

Causes of Test Anxiety

While we often think of anxiety as an uncontrollable emotional state, it can actually be caused by simple, practical things. One of the most common causes of test anxiety is that a person does not feel adequately prepared for their test. This feeling can be the result of many different issues such as poor study habits or lack of organization, but the most common culprit is time management. Starting to study too late, failing to organize your study time to cover all of the material, or being distracted while you study will mean that you're not well prepared for the test. This may lead to cramming the night before, which will cause you to be physically and mentally exhausted for the test. Poor time management also contributes to feelings of stress, fear, and hopelessness as you realize you are not well prepared but don't know what to do about it.

Other times, test anxiety is not related to your preparation for the test but comes from unresolved fear. This may be a past failure on a test, or poor performance on tests in general. It may come from comparing yourself to others who seem to be performing better or from the stress of living up to expectations. Anxiety may be driven by fears of the future—how failure on this test would affect your educational and career goals. These fears are often completely irrational, but they can still negatively impact your test performance.

> **Review Video: 3 Reasons You Have Test Anxiety**
> Visit mometrix.com/academy and enter code: 428468

Elements of Test Anxiety

As mentioned earlier, test anxiety is considered to be an emotional state, but it has physical and mental components as well. Sometimes you may not even realize that you are suffering from test anxiety until you notice the physical symptoms. These can include trembling hands, rapid heartbeat, sweating, nausea, and tense muscles. Extreme anxiety may lead to fainting or vomiting. Obviously, any of these symptoms can have a negative impact on testing. It is important to recognize them as soon as they begin to occur so that you can address the problem before it damages your performance.

> **Review Video: 3 Ways to Tell You Have Test Anxiety**
> Visit mometrix.com/academy and enter code: 927847

The mental components of test anxiety include trouble focusing and inability to remember learned information. During a test, your mind is on high alert, which can help you recall information and stay focused for an extended period of time. However, anxiety interferes with your mind's natural processes, causing you to blank out, even on the questions you know well. The strain of testing during anxiety makes it difficult to stay focused, especially on a test that may take several hours. Extreme anxiety can take a huge mental toll, making it difficult not only to recall test information but even to understand the test questions or pull your thoughts together.

> **Review Video: How Test Anxiety Affects Memory**
> Visit mometrix.com/academy and enter code: 609003

Effects of Test Anxiety

Test anxiety is like a disease—if left untreated, it will get progressively worse. Anxiety leads to poor performance, and this reinforces the feelings of fear and failure, which in turn lead to poor performances on subsequent tests. It can grow from a mild nervousness to a crippling condition. If allowed to progress, test anxiety can have a big impact on your schooling, and consequently on your future.

Test anxiety can spread to other parts of your life. Anxiety on tests can become anxiety in any stressful situation, and blanking on a test can turn into panicking in a job situation. But fortunately, you don't have to let anxiety rule your testing and determine your grades. There are a number of relatively simple steps you can take to move past anxiety and function normally on a test and in the rest of life.

> **Review Video: How Test Anxiety Impacts Your Grades**
> Visit mometrix.com/academy and enter code: 939819

Physical Steps for Beating Test Anxiety

While test anxiety is a serious problem, the good news is that it can be overcome. It doesn't have to control your ability to think and remember information. While it may take time, you can begin taking steps today to beat anxiety.

Just as your first hint that you may be struggling with anxiety comes from the physical symptoms, the first step to treating it is also physical. Rest is crucial for having a clear, strong mind. If you are tired, it is much easier to give in to anxiety. But if you establish good sleep habits, your body and mind will be ready to perform optimally, without the strain of exhaustion. Additionally, sleeping well helps you to retain information better, so you're more likely to recall the answers when you see the test questions.

Getting good sleep means more than going to bed on time. It's important to allow your brain time to relax. Take study breaks from time to time so it doesn't get overworked, and don't study right before bed. Take time to rest your mind before trying to rest your body, or you may find it difficult to fall asleep.

> **Review Video: <u>The Importance of Sleep for Your Brain</u>**
> Visit mometrix.com/academy and enter code: 319338

Along with sleep, other aspects of physical health are important in preparing for a test. Good nutrition is vital for good brain function. Sugary foods and drinks may give a burst of energy but this burst is followed by a crash, both physically and emotionally. Instead, fuel your body with protein and vitamin-rich foods.

Also, drink plenty of water. Dehydration can lead to headaches and exhaustion, especially if your brain is already under stress from the rigors of the test. Particularly if your test is a long one, drink water during the breaks. And if possible, take an energy-boosting snack to eat between sections.

> **Review Video: <u>How Diet Can Affect your Mood</u>**
> Visit mometrix.com/academy and enter code: 624317

Along with sleep and diet, a third important part of physical health is exercise. Maintaining a steady workout schedule is helpful, but even taking 5-minute study breaks to walk can help get your blood pumping faster and clear your head. Exercise also releases endorphins, which contribute to a positive feeling and can help combat test anxiety.

When you nurture your physical health, you are also contributing to your mental health. If your body is healthy, your mind is much more likely to be healthy as well. So take time to rest, nourish your body with healthy food and water, and get moving as much as possible. Taking these physical steps will make you stronger and more able to take the mental steps necessary to overcome test anxiety.

Mental Steps for Beating Test Anxiety

Working on the mental side of test anxiety can be more challenging, but as with the physical side, there are clear steps you can take to overcome it. As mentioned earlier, test anxiety often stems from lack of preparation, so the obvious solution is to prepare for the test. Effective studying may be the most important weapon you have for beating test anxiety, but you can and should employ several other mental tools to combat fear.

First, boost your confidence by reminding yourself of past success—tests or projects that you aced. If you're putting as much effort into preparing for this test as you did for those, there's no reason you should expect to fail here. Work hard to prepare; then trust your preparation.

Second, surround yourself with encouraging people. It can be helpful to find a study group, but be sure that the people you're around will encourage a positive attitude. If you spend time with others who are anxious or cynical, this will only contribute to your own anxiety. Look for others who are motivated to study hard from a desire to succeed, not from a fear of failure.

Third, reward yourself. A test is physically and mentally tiring, even without anxiety, and it can be helpful to have something to look forward to. Plan an activity following the test, regardless of the outcome, such as going to a movie or getting ice cream.

When you are taking the test, if you find yourself beginning to feel anxious, remind yourself that you know the material. Visualize successfully completing the test. Then take a few deep, relaxing breaths and return to it. Work through the questions carefully but with confidence, knowing that you are capable of succeeding.

Developing a healthy mental approach to test taking will also aid in other areas of life. Test anxiety affects more than just the actual test—it can be damaging to your mental health and even contribute to depression. It's important to beat test anxiety before it becomes a problem for more than testing.

> **Review Video: Test Anxiety and Depression**
> Visit mometrix.com/academy and enter code: 904704

Study Strategy

Being prepared for the test is necessary to combat anxiety, but what does being prepared look like? You may study for hours on end and still not feel prepared. What you need is a strategy for test prep. The next few pages outline our recommended steps to help you plan out and conquer the challenge of preparation.

STEP 1: SCOPE OUT THE TEST

Learn everything you can about the format (multiple choice, essay, etc.) and what will be on the test. Gather any study materials, course outlines, or sample exams that may be available. Not only will this help you to prepare, but knowing what to expect can help to alleviate test anxiety.

STEP 2: MAP OUT THE MATERIAL

Look through the textbook or study guide and make note of how many chapters or sections it has. Then divide these over the time you have. For example, if a book has 15 chapters and you have five days to study, you need to cover three chapters each day. Even better, if you have the time, leave an extra day at the end for overall review after you have gone through the material in depth.

If time is limited, you may need to prioritize the material. Look through it and make note of which sections you think you already have a good grasp on, and which need review. While you are studying, skim quickly through the familiar sections and take more time on the challenging parts. Write out your plan so you don't get lost as you go. Having a written plan also helps you feel more in control of the study, so anxiety is less likely to arise from feeling overwhelmed at the amount to cover.

STEP 3: GATHER YOUR TOOLS

Decide what study method works best for you. Do you prefer to highlight in the book as you study and then go back over the highlighted portions? Or do you type out notes of the important information? Or is it helpful to make flashcards that you can carry with you? Assemble the pens, index cards, highlighters, post-it notes, and any other materials you may need so you won't be distracted by getting up to find things while you study.

If you're having a hard time retaining the information or organizing your notes, experiment with different methods. For example, try color-coding by subject with colored pens, highlighters, or post-it notes. If you learn better by hearing, try recording yourself reading your notes so you can listen while in the car, working out, or simply sitting at your desk. Ask a friend to quiz you from your flashcards, or try teaching someone the material to solidify it in your mind.

STEP 4: CREATE YOUR ENVIRONMENT

It's important to avoid distractions while you study. This includes both the obvious distractions like visitors and the subtle distractions like an uncomfortable chair (or a too-comfortable couch that makes you want to fall asleep). Set up the best study environment possible: good lighting and a comfortable work area. If background music helps you focus, you may want to turn it on, but otherwise keep the room quiet. If you are using a computer to take notes, be sure you don't have any other windows open, especially applications like social media, games, or anything else that could distract you. Silence your phone and turn off notifications. Be sure to keep water close by so you stay hydrated while you study (but avoid unhealthy drinks and snacks).

Also, take into account the best time of day to study. Are you freshest first thing in the morning? Try to set aside some time then to work through the material. Is your mind clearer in the afternoon or evening? Schedule your study session then. Another method is to study at the same time of day that you will take the test, so that your brain gets used to working on the material at that time and will be ready to focus at test time.

STEP 5: STUDY!

Once you have done all the study preparation, it's time to settle into the actual studying. Sit down, take a few moments to settle your mind so you can focus, and begin to follow your study plan. Don't give in to distractions or let yourself procrastinate. This is your time to prepare so you'll be ready to fearlessly approach the test. Make the most of the time and stay focused.

Of course, you don't want to burn out. If you study too long you may find that you're not retaining the information very well. Take regular study breaks. For example, taking five minutes out of every hour to walk briskly, breathing deeply and swinging your arms, can help your mind stay fresh.

As you get to the end of each chapter or section, it's a good idea to do a quick review. Remind yourself of what you learned and work on any difficult parts. When you feel that you've mastered the material, move on to the next part. At the end of your study session, briefly skim through your notes again.

But while review is helpful, cramming last minute is NOT. If at all possible, work ahead so that you won't need to fit all your study into the last day. Cramming overloads your brain with more information than it can process and retain, and your tired mind may struggle to recall even previously learned information when it is overwhelmed with last-minute study. Also, the urgent nature of cramming and the stress placed on your brain contribute to anxiety. You'll be more likely to go to the test feeling unprepared and having trouble thinking clearly.

So don't cram, and don't stay up late before the test, even just to review your notes at a leisurely pace. Your brain needs rest more than it needs to go over the information again. In fact, plan to finish your studies by noon or early afternoon the day before the test. Give your brain the rest of the day to relax or focus on other things, and get a good night's sleep. Then you will be fresh for the test and better able to recall what you've studied.

STEP 6: TAKE A PRACTICE TEST

Many courses offer sample tests, either online or in the study materials. This is an excellent resource to check whether you have mastered the material, as well as to prepare for the test format and environment.

Check the test format ahead of time: the number of questions, the type (multiple choice, free response, etc.), and the time limit. Then create a plan for working through them. For example, if you have 30 minutes to take a 60-question test, your limit is 30 seconds per question. Spend less time on the questions you know well so that you can take more time on the difficult ones.

If you have time to take several practice tests, take the first one open book, with no time limit. Work through the questions at your own pace and make sure you fully understand them. Gradually work up to taking a test under test conditions: sit at a desk with all study materials put away and set a timer. Pace yourself to make sure you finish the test with time to spare and go back to check your answers if you have time.

After each test, check your answers. On the questions you missed, be sure you understand why you missed them. Did you misread the question (tests can use tricky wording)? Did you forget the information? Or was it something you hadn't learned? Go back and study any shaky areas that the practice tests reveal.

Taking these tests not only helps with your grade, but also aids in combating test anxiety. If you're already used to the test conditions, you're less likely to worry about it, and working through tests until you're scoring well gives you a confidence boost. Go through the practice tests until you feel comfortable, and then you can go into the test knowing that you're ready for it.

Test Tips

On test day, you should be confident, knowing that you've prepared well and are ready to answer the questions. But aside from preparation, there are several test day strategies you can employ to maximize your performance.

First, as stated before, get a good night's sleep the night before the test (and for several nights before that, if possible). Go into the test with a fresh, alert mind rather than staying up late to study.

Try not to change too much about your normal routine on the day of the test. It's important to eat a nutritious breakfast, but if you normally don't eat breakfast at all, consider eating just a protein bar. If you're a coffee drinker, go ahead and have your normal coffee. Just make sure you time it so that the caffeine doesn't wear off right in the middle of your test. Avoid sugary beverages, and drink enough water to stay hydrated but not so much that you need a restroom break 10 minutes into the test. If your test isn't first thing in the morning, consider going for a walk or doing a light workout before the test to get your blood flowing.

Allow yourself enough time to get ready, and leave for the test with plenty of time to spare so you won't have the anxiety of scrambling to arrive in time. Another reason to be early is to select a good seat. It's helpful to sit away from doors and windows, which can be distracting. Find a good seat, get out your supplies, and settle your mind before the test begins.

When the test begins, start by going over the instructions carefully, even if you already know what to expect. Make sure you avoid any careless mistakes by following the directions.

Then begin working through the questions, pacing yourself as you've practiced. If you're not sure on an answer, don't spend too much time on it, and don't let it shake your confidence. Either skip it and come back later, or eliminate as many wrong answers as possible and guess among the remaining ones. Don't dwell on these questions as you continue—put them out of your mind and focus on what lies ahead.

Be sure to read all of the answer choices, even if you're sure the first one is the right answer. Sometimes you'll find a better one if you keep reading. But don't second-guess yourself if you do immediately know the answer. Your gut instinct is usually right. Don't let test anxiety rob you of the information you know.

If you have time at the end of the test (and if the test format allows), go back and review your answers. Be cautious about changing any, since your first instinct tends to be correct, but make sure you didn't misread any of the questions or accidentally mark the wrong answer choice. Look over any you skipped and make an educated guess.

At the end, leave the test feeling confident. You've done your best, so don't waste time worrying about your performance or wishing you could change anything. Instead, celebrate the successful completion of this test. And finally, use this test to learn how to deal with anxiety even better next time.

Review Video: <u>5 Tips to Beat Test Anxiety</u>
Visit mometrix.com/academy and enter code: 570656

Important Qualification

Not all anxiety is created equal. If your test anxiety is causing major issues in your life beyond the classroom or testing center, or if you are experiencing troubling physical symptoms related to your anxiety, it may be a sign of a serious physiological or psychological condition. If this sounds like your situation, we strongly encourage you to seek professional help.

Thank You

We at Mometrix would like to extend our heartfelt thanks to you, our friend and patron, for allowing us to play a part in your journey. It is a privilege to serve people from all walks of life who are unified in their commitment to building the best future they can for themselves.

The preparation you devote to these important testing milestones may be the most valuable educational opportunity you have for making a real difference in your life. We encourage you to put your heart into it—that feeling of succeeding, overcoming, and yes, conquering will be well worth the hours you've invested.

We want to hear your story, your struggles and your successes, and if you see any opportunities for us to improve our materials so we can help others even more effectively in the future, please share that with us as well. **The team at Mometrix would be absolutely thrilled to hear from you!** So please, send us an email (support@mometrix.com) and let's stay in touch.

> **If you'd like some additional help, check out these other resources we offer for your exam:**
> **http://MometrixFlashcards.com/Series79**

Additional Bonus Material

Due to our efforts to try to keep this book to a manageable length, we've created a link that will give you access to all of your additional bonus material:

mometrix.com/bonus948/series79